When A Man Prays

The Lion and the Lamb
Must ARISE

Devon & Maria Harbajan

Foreword by Bishop Neville Owens

WHEN A MAN PRAYS
The Lion and the Lamb Must ARISE
Copyright © 2016 Devon & Maria Harbajan

ISBN 978-976-95940-4-3

Cover Art by Dale Sewell

Published by: The Publisher's Notebook Ltd

                  Email: publisher@thepublishersnotebook.com

Printed in Jamaica

Dedication

We affectionately dedicate this book to our beloved son, DeMario S. Harbajan, who loves Jesus, and is a young worshipper, intercessor and lover of the Word of God. We also dedicate this book to every godson we have, praying that you will all grow up to be men of God and certainly men of prayer.

To every man of God and all the Men of Prayer who have influenced us from the time we were Christians in our youth. We pray for special blessings upon those who taught us how to pray, who corrected us when we made mistakes in the act of praying, and who recognized our call and ministry of prayer. Thank you for giving to the Lord. Our lives have been transformed as a result.

Acknowledgements

We wish to express our deepest appreciation to all the men of prayer who helped us to write this book through their candid sharing and answering the questions that we asked in our seeking to understand and assist other men of prayer to ARISE.

To Bishop Peter Morgan, Lt. Col. Raphael Mason, Rev. Newton Gabbidon and others who influenced us as men of prayer, opening up to us the importance of praying for our nation.

To all the men who have served faithfully through the years that NIPNOJ has been established. You are Family. Thanks for your service and support which has been invaluable.

To the following persons who contributed in sharing their opinions and views which helped to increase our understanding of men in prayer:

Pastors Mark Dawes, Timon Williamson, David Henry and Daniel Alonge.

Robert Edwards, Mwando Townsend, Courtnay Hunter, and O. Stephen Peart.

"When a man prays, the Lion and the Lamb must ARISE- and the women are protected and cherished."

Devon & Maria Harbajan

Contents

Foreword

As a student of prayer, I am deeply grateful, humbled and privileged to write the foreword to such a masterly and timely work on prayer, written by two generals of prayer.

The authors, Revs. Devon and Maria Harbajan have over 40 years combined in the prayer ministry of the church, locally, regionally and internationally. Together they have taught and most importantly, modeled prayer, helping to foster an end time prayer revival.

Rev. Devon Harbajan writes: "There was something that drove David into the presence of the Lord…and it's the same thing that I have seen motivating men who have cultivated a serious prayer life. This motivating factor is a panting after God." You will be moved time and time again with clear insight, testimonies of men who are prayer warriors and challenged into a life of prayer.

In these eight chapters, replete with scriptures and quotations from other prayer warriors, there is a passion to be transferred to waiting hearts and minds. Truly this work is a provoker to every "pregnant" man and woman, who carries the burden of the Lord for the nation(s). The time has come for every praying man and woman to arise and be enlisted in this great end time army.

I therefore highly recommend this book as a must have and a must read to every serious student of prayer as he/she seeks to fulfill the threefold ministry of the greatest intercessor, Jesus Christ, that of Prophet, Priest and King.

[Bishop Neville Owens (JP), founder, Love and Faith World Outreach Ministries and the Mizpah School of Intercessors; Coordinator – Caribbean Region of Ministers' Prayer Network]

.

Preface

We did not choose this topic. The topic chose us. It came by inspiration that we should write a book examining the issues that males might have and why they do not seem to be flocking the prayer rooms and prayer ministries. Beyond the gatherings, they don't seem able to get it together in their personal prayer lives. The discipline of praying consistently seems to elude many. Another reason is the fact that women are crying out for men to return to the forefront of the battle.

Even if women have fought in some nations and in certain dispensations of their lives for liberation, they, especially in the Church, have hungered for male leadership in the home and within the Body of Christ. Women have come to the counselling room utterly frustrated and exhausted from having to carry the family spiritually when there is a male heading the household. Marriages are being negatively affected because Christian women had dreamt of the ideal of marrying a Christian who will lead them into spiritual things. They ended up, however, having to rescue their children spiritually because the spiritual leader in the home abandoned his post.

Another reason for this book is a simple one. We miss our men, especially when they are not being the leaders that we know that they are born to be. We grieve when they are not maximizing the potential that God as deposited in them as priests, intercessors and king. Since God created women and gave them the gift and ability to be "help-mates", then we believe the Holy Spirit can use women to sensitively encourage the men in their lives, even the little ones, the children, to become ALL that God has created them to be.

This book then is to help men to understand themselves, to gain insight into how the difference in gender, how they see prayer, how they experience prayer, personally and corporately, may be affecting their fervency, frequency and potency in praying. Then having understood these things, not to make an excuse for a lukewarm or absent prayer life, but instead to ARISE and become everything that God intended them to be. Instead to lead from the forefront of the battle. Instead to roar like, and release the ferocity, strength and courage of a lion in the face of the enemy; to pray and act as God bids them to in order to bring reformation in their nation and transformation in their Churches. It is also to help the women who love them and want to encourage them in their understanding as well, so they can be truly one in this critical area of their relationship with God and each other.

Men too are crying out. They are feeling weak spiritually; unable to meet the task of leading their families like men of old. They see the frustration in their spouses and sometimes respond with intense negative emotions or plain withdrawal. Deep inside however, they cry for help. It is a silent cry born out of an innate knowledge that there is more to them than what they are experiencing and what their loved ones are seeing, but God has heard and is responding. Now is the time and the season is here. Men are rising up not just to their fatherly role in assisting in the physical nurturing of their children but in washing their wives with the Word. They are teaching their children to love the Lord their God with all of their heart, soul and mind. They are rising up to be the warriors, conquerors and the victors that they are. They are arising to be intercessors and priests in their home, standing between their families and the forces of the world and of darkness that seek to devour them. May ALL of God's Men ARISE in this hour and take their place in the forefront of the battle being undergirded throughout by prayer.

Evangelist Kernel Williams, a faithful Man of Prayer, interceding for the Nation at Intercessors Mobilization Camp, 2015

Introduction

Maria:

In one of the companies that I counsel, I have had an awesome privilege of counseling men. Apart from having a husband who is not afraid to expose his heart to me, this is the experience which has given me an insight into the fact that men experience much of the same feelings as women do; become damaged in similar ways when their hearts are broken, when they are disappointed or when they are afraid. They back down and back off and withdraw into their "caves" to protect their hearts. They get wounded like women do and are fearful in many ways but usually express their emotions differently.

The Holy Spirit Himself gave me this insight by revelation about ten years ago. He pointed out that men cry **inside** ten times as much as women. I shared it that evening with a group of intercessors of both genders and asked the men there if this was true. One African brother stood up, confirmed the revelation and explained it in such a way that his words have stuck with me. *"When we are backed into a corner; our backs against a wall, feeling helpless and trapped, we come out fighting and some become violent!"* Men feel the need to fight their way out and that sometimes leads to others getting hurt in the process. Men experience hurt deeply. They feel emotional pain and are often confused about what to do with these feelings. Those who do not "hurt" others

> Men have been under serious attack from the Enemy of their souls to remain in the background when it comes to spiritual things. They have been drawn away, even enticed by the powers of darkness to not get involved in church work.

shut down, that is they go into their "cave" or end their own lives!

5

What does this reality have to do with men in prayer? This retreating, this suppression of the warrior and fighter within our Christian males, especially if prolonged can affect them adversely. This does not only happen in their relating to others in a biblical way but ultimately in their prayer walk. It is full time that husbands, sons, fathers, church brothers be encouraged and taught how to come out of their "caves" and release the warrior in them in order to lead their family and church the way God intended.

We must be awakened to the fact that although we all pray, there is a distinctive feature to note. Men and women are structured differently and this impacts on our prayer life. Prayer may be approached differently by each gender but has similar effect in advancing God's kingdom and destroying the kingdom of darkness. In my three decades of being an intercessor, I have noted this distinction but never quite paused to investigate it until God mandated us to write this book. Where do we start? The answer was to seek to understand the differences between men and women in intercession and whether or not these differences affect the prayers of our men in practice, method and impact. This we did by asking the men themselves – men who pray. Our decades being involved in the prayer ministry and leading men have taught us much, but it is interesting to hear the opinions of those who have also struggled over the years in the place of prayer. We found their comments to be insightful and helpful as we build a case for men rising up in prayer at this time. If there is a time that we need strong men of prayer in the family, Church and nation, it is now.

Men have been under serious attack from the enemy of their souls to remain in the background when it comes to spiritual things. They have been drawn away, even enticed by the powers of darkness to not get involved in church work. Some have lost their joy in serving God or have been turned off by what they see happening in the churches. Prayer then has been dominated by women but there has been a missing link – our men! There is a void that has been left and felt when engaging in spiritual warfare without men. Why? Something happens when men roar in the face of the enemy! This is because God created man to have dominion and rule over His creation (Genesis 1:28-29). The enemy usurped this authority by deception, (Genesis 3) but even then God still gave man authority and power over the devil.

> "*And I will put enmity between you and the woman and between your offspring and hers; he will crush your head and you will strike his feet*" (Gen 3:15)

Satan is fully aware that man has the authority to crush his head. When you crush the head of a snake it dies. However all Satan has authority to do is to strike our feet. So when men roar in the face of the Enemy and exercise their authority to step on his head in spiritual warfare, he gets an instant, fatal headache.

It is no wonder that the Scripture says:

> "*I have written to you, fathers, because you know Him who has been from the beginning. I have written to you, young men, because you are strong, and the word of God abides in you, and you have overcome the evil one.*" *(1 John 2:14 – NASB*)

The Enemy has to be afraid of and try in every way to keep down the male gender if the Scripture is declaring them as "*strong*", declaring that they "*have overcome the evil one*", and that they *shall crush the enemy's head*. These Scriptures alone could be a strong encouragement to Christian men who are currently feeling weak in the face of the Enemy. God calls men strong. This might not be an innate strength, or one that they recognize, but it is certainly a strength that God empowers the male gender with to step in the neck of the enemy. When they rise up in that strength, they become like David, men after His own heart. Which male believer would not want this commendation of God – "*a man after My own heart." (Acts 13:22)*

Chapter One

Isn't It Astounding to Hear a Man Pray?

If one Jacob can prevail over the angel, then what could several Jacobs accomplish? In the prayer meeting, as nowhere else, are Christian graces thus brought together with powerful reactionary and reflective force.

J. B. Johnston

Maria

It all began in July 1991. I was a part of a team of three intercessors from Jamaica, joined by another Jamaican intercessor-leader who was a resident in New York, headed for Lagos, Nigeria. The mission was to represent the Caribbean region and the Afro-descendants at a Conference to deal with the issue of slavery and its far-reaching effects across the globe. There were areas in West Africa where the trade was carried on that still were not prospering, e.g. Badagry, which was visited by the attendees. We were taken on an official visit to this site where we made intercession to lift the curses on the land. We beheld the chains used on all parts of the body, including the neck. It was difficult to listen to the African guide giving us the details of how persons were captured and chained but we kept our focus for the journey, which was to break curses.

The West Africans sensed that the Afro-descendants were also still reeling from a sense of being "displaced" from their Motherland and struggling with feelings of inferiority in their family and professional lives right across the globe. The Conference also had Europeans representing their forefathers, the instigators and primary beneficiaries of the slave trade. I use the term primary, since I learnt for the first time that the West Africans, upon their own admission to us and by issuing a

8

public apology which shocked us to the core, bore great responsibility for the success of such a trade. They admitted and held themselves accountable because they were the ones who "sold" their brothers and sisters to the white buyers, for material gain! This is not conjecture. This was never stressed to me while studying black history in school but the West Africans took responsibility before God for their part in that act. I remember wondering as they apologized to us, who were representing the Afro-descendants, if we should transfer the anger that we had long felt for the white slave-owners to them! However, it was neither the time nor the occasion for bitterness but apology, forgiveness and release of the guilty ones.

This was the primary reason for this trip which took us almost a two-day's journey across many oceans. As I sat, listened and observed, it struck me that there was a second major impact taking place on my life. The Conference was hosted by Intercessors For Africa which was led at the time by Emeka Nwampka, a Nigerian. Bro. Emeka was the one who had issued the invitation to us to attend as representatives from the Caribbean. This was after he was invited by the National Intercessory Prayer Network of Jamaica to do an all-island intercessory tour, stopping in each of the parishes to minister and to do critical intercession. I was privileged to be a part of the team from NIPNOJ that accompanied him. At the Conference in Africa, after each teaching session, there was heavy praying and primarily by men! Yes, the Conference had hundreds of attendees and many were women but when it came time for prayer, strong black African men came to the front of the meeting place, held their fists in the air and made strong petitions to God. I was completely surprised and very distracted! I had never seen this – so many men leading in prayer from the front, in the congregation! These were men who obviously knew how to talk to God; how to do combat with the forces of darkness and who were very aware that they needed to lead from the frontline in prayer. Their voices rose in a crescendo, thundering up to the heavens with a passion, authority and power that refused to be ignored. I watched as the men on the platform led, with scores of men who automatically came forward, getting closer to the platform when it was time to pray. Another thing that struck me was how they obediently responded when the person at the mike, said, in "Jesus Name, Amen".

9

Silence followed and the meeting moved on to the next item. It was like a well laid out army!

One might be wondering, well, did I not have men in Jamaica who led in prayer? Yes I did and I have been to many prayer meetings in Jamaica and all over the world. However, up until this day, over two decades after, I have not been in a prayer meeting, where all the men, not just a leader, stepped in the frontline and prayed like generals and officers in an army. That African experience left an indelible imprint upon my soul, and a longing for God's men everywhere to arise and take their place in the frontline of the battle in spiritual warfare.

It is interesting that while attending that conference, we were taken to the market in Lagos to purchase some items. It was near 3:00p.m. The team heard scuffling and there was uproar with men running from their stalls. We quickly asked our host what was happening, wondering if we needed to take evasive action. Our calm host smiled and responded, "They are just getting ready for prayer". "So they leave their stalls unattended to go and pray?" one of us asked. The answer was in the affirmative.

When we turned to look, we saw a wide open space in the market and what looked like approximately 200 men kneeling on the ground, bowing and praying. They were Muslims. Again I was struck by the fact that men can humble themselves and pray but this left me with a puzzling question. Why weren't God's men, everywhere, humbling themselves in a similar fashion; leaving behind what mattered to them, their livelihood, to spend time in prayer. These two pictures have not left my mind as I have longed to see strong men of God, if not literally, at least figuratively, bowing their knees before God in prayer! As I have yearned to see, in my own nation, prayer, not being seen as a "women's thing". I have long been a little disturbed by the term, 'Prayer Mothers', especially because I have never heard of a band of praying men in a congregation, being given the title 'Prayer Fathers'. In all the prayer meetings I have been to over three decades, I have not seen a group of men, seated in a particular area designated for the male watchmen-intercessors in that fellowship; in the same way I have seen it done for the females.

Does the Bible make a distinction between when a man prays and when a woman does? Not directly, because we have the same access to the Throne of Grace, we are heard by God in like manner and we have the assurance of answered prayer if we adhere to God's standards. We can however, come to some conclusions by studying men who prayed in the bible and bible references to men and their position of authority especially in spiritual warfare.

The Plight of the Male Seed

We have often wondered if there is not a diabolical plan even in modern times to annihilate the male seed, if not literally, at least in their effectiveness in their homes, churches and within the society. We look at our prisons, our fatherless homes, the bodies hanging out on street corners, the abuse of drugs, the amount of insane persons on the streets, etc. and who do we see in front and high on the statistics? Males. Yes, our sons, our fathers and brothers who seem destined for destruction. Within the Church, the few male heads seen poses a question. Why aren't the male seed in church more? Why have many of them run away from their domestic responsibilities? Why does it seem like they are under such oppression and demonic attack? This is not a modern-day phenomenon. History, including Bible history points to this malady and therefore could help us to draw some conclusions.

In Exodus 1 and also in Matthew 2:16, we see a diabolical plan to get rid of the male seed.

> *Then the king of Egypt spoke to the Hebrew midwives, one of whom was named Shiphrah and the other was named Puah; and he said, "When you are helping the Hebrew women to give birth and see them upon the birthstool, if it is a son, then you shall put him to death; but if it is a daughter, then she shall live." But the midwives feared God, and did not do as the king of*

11

Egypt had commanded them, but let the boys live Exodus 1:15-17 (NASB)

Then Herod, when he saw that he was deceived by the wise men, was exceedingly angry; and he sent forth and put to death all the male children who were in Bethlehem and in all its districts, from two years old and under, according to the time which he had determined from the wise men. Matthew 2:16 (NKJV)

Both national leaders wanted to ensure that the male seed at a certain age were wiped out. In both instances they were seen as a threat! Both rulers chose this method in order to deal with their own fears. The Enemy already knew that ONE was among them who would emerge as a strong leader and challenge the powers that be. In the Old Testament it was Moses and in the New Testament, Jesus. On both occasions however, the answer for those in authority was the annihilation of the males! King Herod had an option but instead of Herod searching, and narrowing the search until that One was found, he was demonically inspired to destroy all the sons! This is not a coincidence. There is something within the male seed that is a threat to the Enemy of our souls and his forces of darkness. That threat is the authority to crush the head of the Enemy.

The demoniac in the Gadarenes in *Luke 8:27 – 39 (NASB)* is a prime example of what Satan has done and continues to do to our male seed. Let's look at this passage closely and see what the Holy Spirit reveals.

And when He came out onto the land, He was met by a man from the city who was possessed with demons; and who had not put on any clothing for a long time, and was not living in a house, but in the tombs. (v 27)

Firstly, he was naked, exposed not only to the natural elements but to the spiritual ones too. He was uncovered, vulnerable, stripped of his manhood and the dignity that goes along with it. Those demonic forces that had him bound did not care about the embarrassing position they had placed him in. They did not care about the dangers to his health in different climatic conditions. Truth be told; neither are they concerned about the distressing and disconcerting position that many of our men are in in modern times.

This son's place of abode was among the dead! The living among the dead? That just bears out the Scripture that Satan comes to *"steal, kill and destroy" (John 10:10)*. How many times have we seen our men driven to fellowship with "dead" things – the type of situations that will be to their demise? They have been enticed into drugs, women, guns, money laundering, pornography, child-trafficking, incest, etc. Sometimes they know that it could possibly cause them their very lives and everything that they hold dear, but they will run impetuously in the direction of danger because of the "challenge" the situation may invite and the perceived satisfaction that will be achieved. Prov 6:27 tells us that they are actually taking *"burning coal into their chests"*. Many times this satisfaction is only short-term and short-lived but will render them powerless afterwards and they walk around, when Satan is through with them, like the "living-dead". There seems to be a type of "blindness" that Satan has imposed on our male seed that drives them to destruction to which we helplessly watch them succumb. But do we have to?

> *For He had commanded the unclean spirit to come out of the man. For it had seized him many times; and he was bound with chains and shackles and kept under guard, and yet he would break his bonds and be driven by the demon into the desert. (v. 29)*

The man was "driven" by demons. How many times have we seen our sons and our men being driven into sin, debauchery and wickedness? Mothers, wives, siblings and even other males look on in utter dismay and total unbelief that their dearly beloved relative could come to this! They are driven in such a way that they become the laughing-stock of the community and the heart-breaker within the family. Notice that the man was driven into the "desert" –a place where there is little or no productivity and fruit-bearing. He can no longer have the opportunity to make a positive impact within his family or on his society. We have seen mentally ill men on our streets in our nation and have had to lament about the waste of God's creation and the potential that that person might have had! Sometimes they were like this man, naked, driven, unproductive, but this is somebody's child too.

> *And Jesus asked him, "What is your name?" And he said, "Legion"; for many demons had entered him.(v 30)*

A legion is a multitude. This could be between 3000 and 6000 demonic spirits! Can you even wrap your mind around the fact that so many evil spirits could be packed in one person. It is mind-boggling. How come this man was still alive? Try to imagine what would be happening to the parents who would have seen their son in that state. The memories of him in their arms as a babe and the pictures in their minds of him growing up, would be enough to cause them great distress. What could have led to this? Whether or not they could find an explanation, the point is that no human being should end up in such a state and, like on the streets of our nation, the majority of persons seen in similar conditions are the male seed.

> *And the demons came out of the man and entered the swine; and the herd rushed down the steep bank into the lake and was drowned. (v 33)*

That large herd of pigs "committed suicide". That level of torment was unbearable for them and they ended their existence. I can recall statistics showing that a higher rate of suicidal victims is men. The fact is that men are more successful at suicidal attempts. Drs. Natalie Staats Reiss and Mark Dombeck, in looking at suicide statistics wrote:

> *"Men are more likely to commit suicide than women. Researchers suggest that men suffering from depression are more likely to go unrecognized and untreated than women suffering from depression, in part because men may avoid seeking help (viewing it as a*

14

weakness). Men who are depressed are also more likely to have co-occurring alcohol and substance use disorders than women.

Men are more likely than women to use highly lethal methods to commit suicide... a gun, carbon monoxide, to hang themselves, or to jump from a height to commit suicide. " [https://www.mentalhelp.net/articles/suicide-statistics]

Yes, there are more families that have had to deal with grief from the tragic loss of a son who committed suicide, killed someone, maimed someone while driving recklessly or under the influence of alcohol. There are more prisons built for our sons than our daughters. Please do not misunderstand me. We are not seeking for a balance in the statistics so that as many women as men would be affected in these ways. What we are looking at is the stark reality of an endangered gender, a gender under attack, and we are seeking for God's answer to their dilemma.

God's Answer to Their Plight

Jesus left us the perfect example to deal with the predicament and troubles of our male seed. It is divine intervention. It is to drive out, by the power of God, the forces of darkness that have driven our sons into captivity, whatever the nature of that captivity.

The people went out to see what had happened; and they came to Jesus, and found the man from whom the demons had gone out, sitting down at the feet of Jesus, clothed and in his right mind; and they became frightened. (v 35)

What an opposite scenario after the intervention of Jesus into this man's circumstances. He now was clothed, sitting down instead of acting wildly, breaking chains that others had used to restrain him. Now

15

he was in his right mind. This is God's will for our sons and our men; that they be "covered' by Him, sit at His feet in prayer and consistent fellowship and that they operate with self-controlled minds. They can by the power of Almighty God, with some other men and women who would dare to stand in-the-gap and to intercede for them until they find themselves back in the purpose of God for their lives. We need to press into the supernatural for the freedom of our men!

The people reported how the man had been made well (v 36). Our men need to be made well. They need to take up their original positions intended by God – as leaders of their families, leaders in the Church and in the forefront of the battle against Satan. It is interesting that Jesus told him to *"return to your house and describe what great things God has done for you." (v 39)* On his way he might have been spreading the good news to those he met but he was directed to return home.

The family is important to God and need to see their male seed stand in the power of God. It is a known fact that when men are strong leaders within their families, usually the entire family moves in their direction, whether that direction is for good or for bad. Even the bible tells us that the father is the glory of the child. *(Prov. 17:6)* Research has been increasing and a serious look is being taken at policies that have been made downplaying the role of men within the family. Having seen the results of such research which has proven the critical role of men within their families, international policy makers have been challenged to work on new policies.

With the broadening of paternal roles, there is a greater attention being paid to the effects of men's involvement on the well-being of their families. The initial focus of research in this area was on the role of men in the achievement of gender equality and an equal sharing of domestic responsibilities.

Further research centered on programme and policy initiatives designed to engage men in many areas of family life, including in reproductive health, especially family planning as well as maternal and newborn health - with considerable research focusing on paternal
contribution to positive social and education outcomes for children.

"MEN IN FAMILIES and Family Policy in a Changing World"
[http://www.un.org/esa/socdev/family/docs/men-in-families.]

In Exodus chapter 1, the plot is very clear again – destroy the male seed. It is God's response to the midwives who spared the male babies that is instructive to us and indicates how He felt about the whole scenario:

> *But the midwives feared God, and did not do as the king of Egypt commanded them, but saved the male children alive. So the king of Egypt called for the midwives and said to them, "Why have you done this thing, and saved the male children alive? Exodus 1:17-21(NKJV)*

Out of fear of God the midwives disobeyed the governing authority. They feared God more than man. Out of fear of God, we should all resist any forces, be it natural or supernatural, that has any assignments to destroy our men. We should stand against the unseen forces of darkness that have positioned themselves to oppress our sons, husbands and fathers. *(Eph 6:12)* We should be resisting them in deep intercession until the minds of our "sons" are free from the chains that bind them.
I John 2:13, "...I am writing to you, young men, because you have overcome the evil one." Why would John write this and it seems opposite to what we are generally seeing now within and outside of the walls of our churches and homes. One thing we are sure of is that God's Word is true! If God said it then it is so. But how is it so?

Prayer is NOT a 'Woman's Thing'

Devon:
I believe that the Church needs to change the notion that prayer is mainly a woman thing. Men need to take more lead in prayer.

Maria:

I am the first one to agree with this statement. It has been a lonely journey for over two decades leading a national prayer ministry and watching women primarily carrying the weight and burden of prayer for their families, the Church and the nation.

In the earlier years of my ministry, a Pastor, who is now an elderly minister, met me on the streets in the city close to where the ministry's office is situated and remarked to me, "Men don't like women heading up ministries." At that time the founder and president of the national prayer ministry for which I worked full-time had migrated with his family. The mandate had fallen on me to keep the ministry afloat. This minister went on in the conversation to declare that my ministry might not get very far in this nation because of this - the fact that I was a woman leading a ministry which involved men. I left his presence and this conversation thinking. "Is God unfair? Is He unjust? Would He call me to a ministry knowing all of this and leave me to bat on my own?" I prayed. "Lord if this pastor is correct; if there is such a prejudice out there, then it is You who will have to help me!" I continued to walk on the streets of downtown Kingston that day feeling a bit discouraged.

I must confess that for some years following this encounter with that pastor, I wondered about the truth of his statement as I was sometimes slighted when I made a ministry request within the Body of Christ but when a male intercessor-leader made a similar request, he got through. I sometimes wondered when I saw males who began with a ministry led by a woman, leave to go and form their own ministry, leaving the sister to struggle on her own and there was no dispute and disagreement that led to this. If there was even some truth to this statement, I still wondered why ministries that were headed by men had a great following of faithful women and the men who started out with them ended up leaving after a while. The faithful women were left, carrying the burden of prayer. There seem to be a paradox: men might not be taking up their positions, but they do not like to see women taking positions of leadership. Will God allow a nation to suffer if men refuse to step up to the plate? The answer can be gleaned from Judges 4, the story of the only female judge mentioned in the Bible, Deborah, who led a successful counterattack against Jabin, king of Canaan and his military commander Sisera. It is very clear that when God calls men, He expects them to step forward and to fight and to win the war in His strength.

About ten years after my wonderings and struggles, someone moving under a prophetic anointing and an intercessor himself, while praying in a meeting for me, spelt out this prejudice in details. He prophetically declared that the Lord would be my help and will not allow this "prejudice" to be a stumbling block but will accomplish in and through me what He intends to. Wow! There was and probably still is such a prejudice, I concluded, but God will use whoever He wishes, even a donkey to carry out His will. I must have been that "donkey", maybe not God's first choice, but God chose to use who He could find at the time and will continue to do so – He searches for availability.

But what about God's sovereignty and His right to choose whomever He wishes? Can He not choose a woman as His first choice, from the womb, anointing her to carry out a task that may seem to some males and even females, better suited for a male? If God chooses to do so, it should not in any way distract a man from the mission He was called by God to accomplish.

I was ordained into ministry a few years before my husband. What I admired about his response was the total acceptance of the fact that it was God who called me. His consistent support and encouragement from that time has helped me to do wonders for God. I can still remember from the early days until now, him blessing me and sending me off in God's hands and under His covering on ministry assignments locally and overseas. The issue of competition does not come into play when we are doing God's business. I too recognize God's call on Devon's life and keep prodding him to reach his full potential. He is a truly gifted man and his love for the Lord is in fact, amazing.

After walking through some disappointments subsequently to the minister's pronouncements, God placed some faithful men in our weekly intercessory meetings who have stood the test of time and are still standing as intercessors. We have done several times the ARISE Intercessors Course and in the classes of full-time students, there are Ministers of Religion; the majority of which have been men.

In one of our weekly intercessory meetings, two of the male intercessors prayed for the nation. One fell on his face, flat on his belly, in his white shirt, before God. He cried out under a strong anointing for the leaders of the Church across the nation to be led by the Spirit and not by the pride of position. The only thing that was left was for the place to begin to shake. I thought to myself, while he was praying, "there goes a true man of prayer"!

There is something that has troubled me in recent times however, and it is the fact that even fellowships with strong male leaders, could not seem to find men who were strong in prayer. Many of these fellowships had "Prayer Mothers" and not "Prayer Fathers". Sometimes an area in the fellowship was cordoned off for these Prayer Mothers who were usually dressed alike, perhaps for quick identification. I looked but did not see the men. Where were the praying men? Where were the males who God has sought to *"stand in-the-gap"*? *(Ezek. 22:30)* Don't get me wrong. I thank God for these women who have stood in-the-gap and have held up the arms of many Ministers in battle! They have done so too under much duress and I have heard the testimonies of many of our prominent Ministers that if it had not been for these praying women, their ministries would not be as successful. The amount of converts that they received into their fellowships would not be so if these women were not there faithfully praying. So hats off to the faithful prayer mothers! We esteem them under God.

It troubled me however, that a wrong message was being sent, we would think unintentionally, to the next generations, and that message is that "prayer is a woman's thing." We are aware of the Scriptures that exhorts us to *"call for the weeping women"* *(Jer. 9:17)*. Note however, that the prophet who spoke these words was dubbed the "weeping prophet", an intercessor, one who constantly lamented before God for his nation. His counterpart prophets were also intercessors – Isaiah, Ezekiel, Daniel. Where have we gotten this notion that women should carry the burden and brunt of the praying in the Church? We have never seen this mandated in the Scriptures and no one should buy into it. Women, as one minister said to me recently, may be able to bear burdens longer than men, because of their make-up. However, burdens need to be shared. Battles need to be fought with men on the frontline, and victories need to be won with God's power and strength being manifested in men the way He intended it to be.

Can you imagine if our sons saw, like what I saw in Nigeria, West Africa, men of God, many of them, looking to the heavens and praying for their sons, their nation, their families? What impact that would have on the females and other males looking on! What encouragement this would be to wives and mothers! Above this, what Divine approval this would attract!

Rev. Devon Harbajan, Executive Chairman, National Intercessory Prayer Network of Jamaica / Prayer Centre of the Caribbean, interceding for the nation at Intercessors Camp in Jamaica

Chapter Two

When a Man Prays:
The Lion and LAMB Emerge

I was the shyest human ever invented, but I
had a lion inside me that wouldn't shut up
Ingrid Bergman

Devon:

The Lion and The Lamb

As a child, I vividly remember the church, just a stone's throw at the foot of the hill from where I lived, complete with a bell that would toll every Sunday morning, summoning all and sundry to gather in the house of the Lord. I delighted in dashing down the hill to go to Sunday school to hear the word of the Lord, to listen to bible stories and sing songs of praise and worship. I was fascinated by the bible stories and remember thinking of Jesus as the nice gentle person who was always kind, never saying a harsh word, loving children, taking them on His knees and forgiving sinners while always doing good. This image was reinforced by the prevailing pictures of Jesus then and now, a smiling Jesus, arms outstretched, reaching out to everyone. This was very appealing to the child living at the top of the hill who needed a gentle, comforting, reassuring Jesus, patting him on the head and letting him know that Jesus loves him.

However as I grew older and began to face the harsh realities of life, bullies at school, crime and violence, sickness and disease, the meek and gentle Jesus, though still appealing, was no longer sufficient to be the God in whom I could confidently entrust my life and very soul. So I searched the scriptures, studying to show myself approved. I began to see that the Jesus of my childhood was also the Jesus who said "Woe unto you Scribes and Pharisees" and called the religious leaders of the day white-washed sepulchers. It is the same Jesus who will say "depart from me I know you not" to those who, though religious, have not surrendered their lives to Him to do His will.

As I delved deeper into the scriptures, I came to the realization the same "gentle Jesus meek and mild" was the same Jesus that was Omnipotent, Omniscience, and Omnipresent. It was through Him that I could do all things and face all things. It was at His name that every knee will have to bow and every tongue must confess that Jesus Christ is Lord. It was to that Jesus that I turned to at the age of 15 crying out for healing, and was delivered from Rheumatic Fever. I was tired of the monthly injections of penicillin ever since I was diagnosed at the age of 10, the same year I accepted Jesus as my Lord and Saviour. They left me sore and unable to sit properly for at least a week. Since that time I have remained free from any trace of heart disease or complications from that disease. I came to the realization that the bible and indeed God's creation is full of paradoxes, and one of the greatest paradoxes is that of the true nature of Christ.

In Genesis we read that God created man in his own image and likeness. Image means that we look like God. He has hands, feet, head, hair, etc. just like us. Likeness refers to who God is, His intrinsic nature and character, and how he behaves. The bible is a progressive revelation of who God is so that we can indeed be like Him. The ultimate revelation of God was through the manifestation on earth of his Son, Jesus Christ. In John we read:

> In the beginning was the Word, and the Word was with God and the Word was God.

> And the Word was made flesh, and dwelt among us, (and we beheld his glory, the glory as of the only begotten of the Father,) full of grace and truth. (John 1:1, 14 - KJV)

Jesus Christ on earth was the revelation of who God is, His likeness and nature. Jesus said to his disciples who asked "show us the

Father", "He who has seen me has seen the Father" (John 14:8). Did he mean that he was the Father? No, but He meant that He was exactly like His Father and so if we see Him we have seen the Father because the Father is no different. Yet, I believe that as the revelation of Jesus began in the first book of the bible, the greatest revelation of Himself and by extension of ourselves was made in the last book of the bible.

In Revelation we read about John being taken up into heaven and shown what shall happen in the last days. In Chapter 5 we read:

> *And I saw in the right hand of him that sat on the throne a book written within and on the backside, sealed with seven seals.*
>
> *And I saw a strong angel proclaiming with a loud voice, Who is worthy to open the book, and to loose the seals thereof?*
>
> *And no man in heaven, nor in earth, neither under the earth, was able to open the book, neither to look thereon.*
>
> *And I wept much, because no man was found worthy to open and to read the book, neither to look thereon. (Rev 5:1-4 - KJV)*

Imagine the scene. John was caught up to heaven *"in the last days"* He was being shown what would happen prior to the establishment of God's Kingdom on the earth. A book needed to be opened, and though John might not have fully understood what was in that book and what it represented, he knew that for mankind's sake it must be opened. A lot was riding on it. So when no one was found to open the book, he wept. Suddenly an elder said, *"Weep not: behold, the Lion of the tribe of Judah, the Root of David, hath prevailed to open the book, and to loose the seven seals thereof"*

If we were in John's place, we would turn, expecting to see a Lion, magnificent, majestic, strong, fierce, roaring, worthy to take on all challengers and open the book. Imagine our shock when we turn and see a lamb looking as if it had been killed.

> *And I beheld, and, lo, in the midst of the throne and of the four beasts, and in the midst of the elders, stood a Lamb as it had been slain, having seven horns and seven eyes, which are the seven Spirits of God sent forth into all the earth. (Rev 5:6 - KJV)*

Yet I believe that in this paradox lies one of the greatest revelations of the nature and likeness of Jesus, and by extension, the Godhead. If we can understand this, we will also understand ourselves and be better equipped to become the men and women of God that we ought to be. We will be mighty in God, pulling down strongholds and plundering the devil's kingdom.

The Lion and the Lamb Nature in the Godhead

God created mankind to have dominion and rule over the earth he created. In **Genesis 1:28** we read:

> *God blessed them and said to them, "Be fruitful and increase in number; fill the earth and subdue it. Rule over the fish in the sea and the birds in the sky and over every living creature that moves on the ground" (NIV)*

The command was two-fold:

1. To be fruitful and increase in numbers and fill the earth
2. To subdue the earth and rule over every (other) living creature.

To accomplish this, God established different roles for the male man and the "female man". This does not speak to superiority or inferiority as many are quick to infer, but simply different roles, and different functions. The bible said:

> *God created man in His own image, male and female he created them (Gen 1:27).*

26

Therefore, mankind, or male and female when taken together is the full manifestation of the nature and image of God. In the female, God deposited predominantly that aspect of himself, of his nature that would best equip woman to accomplish her specific role and function. That nature is His Lamb nature, what we have come to call the feminine nature. It is that nature of God that is expressed by Jesus in *Matthew 23:37 (NIV):*

> *Jesus cried, "Jerusalem, Jerusalem, you who kill the prophets and stone those sent to you, how often I have longed to gather your children together, as a hen gathers her chicks under her wings, and you were not willing."*

Also in *Isaiah 49:15* (NIV) we see the mother nature of God expressed:

> *Can a mother forget the baby at her breast and have no compassion on the child she has borne? Though she may forget, I will not forget you!*

In the male, God deposited predominantly that aspect of His nature that would best equip man to accomplish his specific role and function. That nature is His Lion nature, what we call the masculine nature. It is that nature of God that is expressed in *Genesis 49:9-10 (NIV)*:

> *Judah is a lion's whelp; From the prey, my son, you have gone up. He couches, he lies down as a lion, And as a lion, who dares rouse him up? Verse 10 tells us, "The sceptre shall not depart from Judah, Nor the ruler's staff from between his feet, Until Shiloh comes, And to him shall be the obedience of the peoples.*

Also *Revelation 5:5 (NIV)*

Then one of the elders said to me, "Do not weep! See, the Lion of the tribe of Judah, the Root of David, has triumphed. He is able to open the scroll and its seven seals.

It is important to note that both males and females have a deposit of both natures of God, the Lion and the Lamb, but one nature dominates more than other in both sexes, and it is that which gives them their distinction. The masculine Lion nature is more associated with the second mandate to rule and have dominion. Hence this nature expresses itself in the need to be the leader, the risk taker, the protector, the provider, the conqueror, to have dominion and exercise that dominion. The feminine Lamb nature is more associated with the first mandate, which is to be fruitful and multiply, to bear children, to nurture and to care for, to sacrifice and expend itself on behalf of their offspring.

Again, I must emphasize that both natures exist in males and females, but one is more pronounced than the other in the expression of the masculine and feminine form. Hence, generally (I know there are exceptions), men also have a strong desire to procreate and have offspring, raise a family, but not as strong a nature to sacrifice self and nurture (Lamb), while women have a strong instinct to protect and provide for their children but not as strong a desire to rule, dominate and be in charge (Lion).

An examination of the physical characteristics of the man and the woman also clearly speaks to the fact that they were each uniquely designed to accomplish their primary function. It is undeniable that the woman was peculiarly designed to receive the fragile fertilized seed of a new human life, nurture, feed and care for it in her womb for nine months, bring it forth into the world, and then continue to nurture, feed and care for it until it becomes sufficiently mature to be weaned. Man on the other hand was created physically to be the hunter, the provider, the ruler, to conquer and dominate God's creation. As such he is naturally stronger, faster, more aggressive and competitive. Again, I am not saying that there aren't some women who are faster and stronger than some men. However, given the same amount of training and practice, the men generally excel over the women in physical activities and similar feats of strength, speed and stamina.

One important point to make here is that although God gave mankind the mandate to rule and dominate the earth he created, he never gave male man and female man the authority to rule and dominate each other. Woman was created to be a suitable assistant for him. Each role is critical to mankind and none makes one superior or inferior. God expects us to function as the Trinity - Father, Son and Holy Spirit - function. The Father is in charge, he rules. The Son and the Holy Spirit work with the Father to execute His will. They are all equal, but their roles differ.

Manifestations and Expressions Of The Lion And The Lamb In Scriptures

In the setting in heaven described in the *Revelation 5* mentioned earlier in this chapter, I do not believe that John was shocked to see the Lamb, because he would have fully understood, from his time with Jesus, that Jesus was the Lion of the Tribe of Judah, the descendant (root) of David. He would have recalled the prophetic blessing spoken by Jacob over his sons:

> *Judah is a lion's whelp: from the prey, my son, thou art*
> *gone up: he stooped down, he couched as a lion, and as*
> *an old lion; who shall rouse him up? The sceptre shall*
> *not depart from Judah, nor a lawgiver from between his*
> *feet, until Shiloh come; and unto him shall the gathering*
> *of the people be. (Genesis 49:9-10)*

John would have also remembered the words spoken about Jesus *"Behold, the lamb of God that taketh away the sins of the world!" (John 1:29)*. He would have been schooled in the synagogues about the significance of Abraham's response to Isaac's question when he was on his way to sacrifice him.

"God will provide himself a lamb for a burnt offering."
The Greek translation of that Hebrew passage is literally
rendered "the God (will) later himself furnish unto a
whole burnt offering, a son." (Genesis 22:2-8).

John would understand the significance of the yearly Passover which points to the day when God would provide a sacrifice for his people and deliver them from their bondage.

Having understood all of that John would realize that contained within the likeness and nature of Christ, the earthly expression of the Father, is the nature of both the Lion and the Lamb. As he reflected on this paradox, on this duality of nature, he would remember the various manifestation of Jesus as the Lamb, gently saying to the woman caught in adultery, *"Then neither do I condemn you, Go now and sin no more." (John 8:11).* This after convicting the self-righteous crowd who was demanding she be stoned to death, of their own sins.

> If we were in John's place, we would turn, expecting to see a Lion, magnificent, majestic, strong, and fierce, roaring, worthy to take on all challengers and open the book. Imagine our shock when we turn and see a lamb looking as if it had been killed

Other manifestations of the Lamb that John would have remembered are:

- The healing of the daughter of the Syro-Phonecian woman of great faith who was willing to be satisfied with just the crumbs from the Lords table so her daughter could be healed. *(Matt 15:21-28)*

- The healing of the woman with the issue of blood, who touched his garment in faith and was healed. She tremblingly admitted to her action, knowing it was unlawful to touch him, since by her issue of blood she was unclean and should not be in any crowd and most of all should not be touching anyone *(Luke 8:40-56)*.
- Jairus, whose daughter was raised from the dead, though the people laughed Jesus to scorn *(Mark 5:21-43)*
- The acceptance of the children when they were being driven away, and setting them in the midst to declare that of such innocence and child-like faith is the Kingdom of God *(Matt 18:1-6)*.
- The woman at the well who should not have been spoken to but rather condemned for her lifestyle, being offered "living water" *(John 4:1-42)*

In all of these cases it was the gentle nature of the Lamb, understanding their needs and circumstances, which prevailed in granting them their request, even when Jesus had every right to refuse.

Of course, the ultimate manifestation of Jesus as the Lamb would be His sacrificial death on the cross, when He could have called twelve legions of angels to His defense if He so desired *(Matt 26:53)*. Yet He chose to die *"as a sheep goeth to the slaughter"*, so that you and I could have the opportunity to become sons of God and joint-heirs of salvation *(Rom 8:16-17, Gal 4:7 - KJV)*. Even then, during the time of His very arrest, the nature of the Lamb was evident in the healing of the ear of His *"enemies"*, the soldier who had come to arrest Him (*Luke 22:50-51*)

John would also have remembered the Lion of Judah, who roared against the hypocrisy of the Scribes and Pharisees and who:

- drove out the money changers and sellers from the temple with a whip (*John 2:15*)
- called the Pharisees white washed graves (*Matt 23:27*)

- defiantly healed on the Sabbath day, such as the man with the withered hand, even though the Scribes and Pharisees insisted it was unlawful and was plotting against Him *(Lk 6:6-11)*
- consistently confronted, exposed and challenged the hypocrisy of the religious leaders of the day who made their followers "twice" the sinners they were *(Matt 23:15)*.

When the Wrong Nature Manifests

Within each of us God has deposited the nature of the Lion and the nature of the Lamb. However many times great damage is done in the body of Christ, to our loved ones and family members by us men because we are Lions when we should be Lambs, roaring when we should be bleating, and we are Lambs when we should be Lions, bleating when we should be roaring. So as husbands we tear our wives and children to shreds as we unleash the nature of the Lion, but meekly, sheepishly succumb to the demands of our jobs, boss or society to compromise our faith and principles.

Let us look at some common examples of inappropriate manifestation of the Lamb and Lion nature by men. These are examples repeated too frequently and consistently in the homes of Christian men, many of whom are pastors, deacons, elders and leaders in their church.

How many times do we promise our children that we are going to doing something special with them on the weekend, or after work, or attend their recital, football game, swim meet or other event significant to them? Then our boss says he would like us to work, or something else comes up. Without any discussion and examination of possible options, we say yes. We go home and our children are upset because we have (yet again) broken our word to them. We lace into them saying how ungrateful they are, and that we are the ones putting food on the table, clothes on their backs, etc. and it is the job that makes it all possible. We might even physically abuse them. Not only have we roared when we should have bleated and bleated when we should have roared, we have seen the job as the source and the boss as the one in charge, not God.

Who is it that is in charge our lives? Is it God or our human authorities?

We are quick to punish our children for the slightest disobedience, yet we daily disobey what God has commanded us to do. We expect and demand submission from our wives but fail to submit our lives fully to God. We are quick to punish, but expect God to understand our shortcomings. We often times give in easily and quickly to the temptations of the devil and the desires of the flesh. We get hooked on gambling, drinking, smoking and pornography. We have adulterous affairs. Yet we are so judgmental and condemning of our sons, our daughters, our wives and others, ready to roar against them and shred them to pieces with our words and actions. Instead of the Lamb expressing itself to the woman caught in adultery, to our children who make mistakes, it is the Lion that roars. However, when we should stand and roar against temptation and sin in our lives we meekly give in like a Lamb going to the slaughter. In *Hebrews 12:4(NIV)* it says *'In your struggle against sin, you have not yet resisted to the point of shedding your blood"* Men of God, God expects us to fight with everything in us to resist sin and temptation even to the point of shedding blood. Yet how easily we fall for the Proverbs 7 woman. *Prov 7:21-23(NIV)* reads:

> *With persuasive words she led him astray; she seduced him with her smooth talk. All at once he followed her like an ox going to the slaughter, like a deer stepping into a noose. Till an arrow pierces his liver, like a bird darting into a snare, little knowing it will cost him his life.*

Prov 5:3-5(NIV) also states

> *For the lips of the adulterous woman drip honey, and her speech is smoother than oil; but in the end she is bitter as gall, sharp as a double-edged sword.*
> *Her feet go down to death; her steps lead straight to the grave*

How often have we heard of men of God destroying their lives and that of their wives and family, because like an ox to the slaughter, we allow sins to entice and lead us to our destruction? It is interesting that the passage used the image of an ox. Just picture in your mind a woman leading an ox by a rope around his neck to the slaughter. The travesty and foolhardiness of it all, is that at any moment the ox is more than strong enough to break away from the woman, yet he willingly goes along to his death, not knowing until it is too late. This is true for us. God has deposited the strength of the LION within us that must be aroused against sin, unrighteousness and temptation in order to break free from sin's stronghold. Are we going to be Lions, meekly walking behind sin to our destruction, when we can easily break free?

The LAMB nature is easily led astray and therefore when it comes to temptation and dealing with sin, it is the LION that must face the temptations of the devil and not the LAMB. *"All we like sheep have gone astray. We have each one gone after his own way"(Is 53:6)*

Joseph is a good example of this. He was the LION to Potiphar's wife when he should have been, resisting her advances and literally fleeing from temptation, and in so doing honored God, thus preserving his life, purpose and calling in God. The Lion arose in him and declared *"How can I do such a wicked thing and sin against God?" (Gen 39)*. In the natural, it might have seemed like he was punished by doing the right thing. However, in God's scheme of things, he was properly positioned to be in a place where his gift as an interpreter of dreams would make room for him and bring him to Pharaoh's attention. As a result, because of his faithfulness, standing in his integrity and allowing the Lion to roar, God preserved his life (he should have died based on the charge against him) and made him ruler over Egypt. His faithfulness to the principles of God caused the fledgling nation of Israel, still in its infancy, to be preserved.

David on the other hand was a LAMB to the temptation of Bathsheba when he should have been the LION like Joseph *(2 Sam 11)*. Like a sheep to the slaughter, he did not resist the temptation of seeing a beautiful woman bathing and gave in to his lustful desires. Instead of roaring like Joseph did *"How then can I do such a wicked thing and sin against God?"(Gen 39:9)*, he showed utter contempt for God *(2 Sam v13b)*, which ultimately ended up with him committing murder and a sword and division coming to his household. As a direct consequence of his sin, his own son rose up against him and he had to flee Jerusalem for a season.

The scripture states *"Like a LAMB being led to the slaughter he opened not his mouth"(Is 53:7)*. This was referring to Christ's willingness in going to Calvary, but it speaks to the general nature of LAMBs that they do not know when they are being taken away to the slaughter and many men have sheepishly follow the devil's frock tail, the

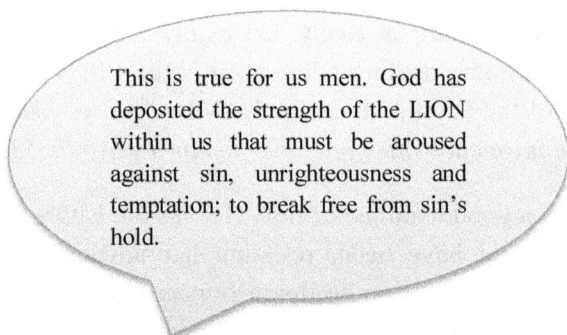

> This is true for us men. God has deposited the strength of the LION within us that must be aroused against sin, unrighteousness and temptation; to break free from sin's hold.

TV and computer screens, to their destruction and that of their families.

Men, be warned and resist the seductive spirits of the women who want to lure you into their arms of destruction. Let the Lion emerge and Roar against them and send them running. Go home to your wives and be the nice cuddly Lambs that will be gentle, caring and affectionate towards them.

From examination of the scriptures I can identify the following situations when the men of God must unleash the Lion in them to withstand the wiles and attacks of the devil. Remember, the Devil goes about "like" a roaring Lion, seeking whom he may devour. However, we are the real deal, we are not **like** a Lion, but we **are** the Lion, through the Lion of the tribe of Judah, Jesus Christ, who is in us.

1. The Lion in us must be unleashed against anything and anyone that seeks to entice, entrap and lead us into sin and away from Christ. No matter how good a friend they are, whether they are our mother, father, brother, sister or relative, no matter how beautiful they appear, we must resist unto death.
2. The Lion in us must be unleashed against anything, anyone, any system that dares to defy God's army, his church and his people. We must not meekly submit, but stand and defend the things of God. We must be jealous concerning the things of God (e.g. David vs Goliath and Jesus vs Satan)
3. The Lion in us must be unleashed against anything that threatens our families and loved ones
4. The Lion in us must be unleashed against anything that violates the laws of God
5. The Lion in us must be unleashed against anything that seeks to establish itself as God and above our God, the King of kings and Lord of Lords
6. The LION is for times of War, the LAMB is for peace. In Revelation, it is the LAMB who will rule after the Lion has conquered.

And I saw no temple therein: for the Lord God Almighty and the Lamb are the temple of it. And the city had no need of the sun, neither of the moon, to shine in it: for the glory of God did lighten it, and the Lamb is the light thereof....And there shall in no wise enter into it any thing that defileth, neither whatsoever worketh abomination, or maketh a lie: but they which are written in the Lamb's Book of Life.(Rev 21:22-27)

What exactly though, is meant by the unleashing of the Lion? Can the Lion be unleashed without wreaking havoc and destruction? This is addressed more fully in the following section, but I must point out here that the unleashing of the Lion in us in not speaking solely to actions and behaviour, but a mindset that we are going to militantly stand and resist the forces of darkness in operation in our families, nation, church and the world under the guidance and leading of the Holy Spirit.

How the Nature of the Lion Must Manifest In Men

The nature of the Lion is strong, powerful, ferocious and proud. The Lion is kingly, a natural leader and hunter. Just the sight of him drives fear in other animals. This nature manifests similarly in men. It is the Lion nature that drives us to be competitive, to want to hunt and conquer women, to take advantage of the weak and seek to dominate everything around us. This LION nature is not evil and was placed in us by God, as I explained earlier, to fulfill God's mandate to have dominion over his creation. However, we need to learn how to properly express and direct this nature. In order to do this, let us look at how we can properly express the Lion in us in the three primary instinctive natures - that of hunter, leader, and competitor.

The Hunter

The hunter nature is that part of us that drives us to be the provider and protector of our families and those dependent on us. When we are not fulfilling this role, we feel useless, unfulfilled and depressed. It is that aspect of us also that makes us pursue and try to win the affections of the opposite sex, seeing such an accomplishment as somewhat of a conquest. It is that aspect of us that fulfills our desire for aggression and ferocity.

In much earlier times, before the advent of modern society, this quality of the male was not only greatly appreciated and demanded, but was essential to survival. The hunter in us was unleashed daily in the hunt for the day's meal, to fight against wild animals and many other threats against the safety of the family. It was like second nature to us and was our primary role and function. The successful hunter, protector and provider was held in high esteem and valued by society.

However, in today's modern society, the hunter is not so much in demand or even seen as relevant anymore. We don't have to hunt for our meals anymore - we just have to walk to the nearest supermarket or fast food outlet. Furthermore, our wives and children no longer have to depend on us for their meals either, they too can just walk to the supermarket or fast food outlet. However, we are still wired to be hunters, we still have the need to express our aggression and ferocity, but there seems to be very few appropriate avenues of expression for this. So instead we become hunters of women, relishing the chase and the conquest, then moving on to the next. We physically abuse our wives and children and take advantage of the weak and helpless. All of this is in an attempt to satisfy the hunter within us.

God has created the hunter to conquer, to fight, compete, and be aggressive. That aggression must be directed against the enemy in intercession, in active lobbying and defending justice and righteousness. It must be used to fight for our children and wives to become all that they can become in Christ. It must be used to protect, nurture and develop them. It must be used to fight for the fatherless and orphans, the many boys and girls who have no father to fight for them. It must be used to fight for the widows and ensure they are not taken advantage of. It must be used to defend the poor, the weak, and the marginalized.

As men of God we need to recognize and understand this aspect of ourselves. We need to recognize who our true enemy and greatest threat is and direct our aggression and ferocity against him. That enemy is the devil, not our wives, not our children, not the government, not politicians, not the police and certainly not our fellow human beings.

> *For we wrestle not against flesh and blood, but against principalities, against powers, against the rulers of the darkness of this world, against spiritual wickedness in high places. (Eph 6:12 KJV)*

Note that the mindset of the hunter is that of the stronger pursuing the weaker, or the fearless pursuing the fearful. We are the stronger, not the weaker *(Greater is He that is in you than he that is in the world – 1 John 4:4 KJV)*, the fearless, not the fearful *(For God has not given us a Spirit of fear, but of love and of power and of sound mind – 2 Tim 1:7)*.

38

How then do we unleash the Lion against this enemy? Below are strategies that I have employed which I have found to be very effective and fulfilling ways to legitimately express the Lion in us. These strategies allow us to be men in the pursuit of Christ without feeling that in addition to surrendering our hearts when we became Christians, we have to surrender our masculinity as well.

Release the Lion:

1)   *In intercession and feeding on the Word of God*. This might seem to be contrary to the nature of the Lion, but is indeed the foundation in properly unleashing the nature of the Lion in us. Before a Lion even starts pursuing its prey, it establishes its presence and ownership of the territory with its roar. It terrifies its prey and causes them to become frightened even before the hunt begins. Frighten animals (and demons) get confused easily and make poor decisions. The Lion's roar also serves as a warning to other lions that they are in another's territory and they are to stay away or will be driven away (or worse). Lastly, the lion's roar is a means of communication, gathering the tribe and rallying them against external threats. Our intercession ought to be the roar of the Lion in us which establishes our presence in our homes, our communities, our workplaces, our schools and our nations. It should terrify the enemy, throwing him into confusion, and serve as a warning that God's kingdom is well represented and that they must stay away. It is also the means by which we communicate in the spiritual realm with our Chief Lion, rallying the Host of Heaven to come to our aid.

When a Lion is pursuing its prey, it takes the time to be quiet, still, watch, stalk, hide and then pounce. In intercession and the study of God's word is the time that we are also quiet, still, watchful. We are listening to the Lord, receiving instructions and strategies, downloading His plan and purpose, not ours. We are stalking and studying the Enemy. Then at the right time, based on God's timing and the leading of the Holy Spirit, emerge from our surveillance in intercession and pounce.

For the weapons of our warfare are
not carnal, but mighty through God

to the pulling down of strong holds;
(2 Cor 10:4)

2)   ***In Evangelism and missions.*** There is no greater area of Christian ministry that demands the Lion in us to come forth than the area of evangelism and missions. The mission fields should be dominated by men, not women. This is where we actively and physically come face to face with the enemy. This is where we deliberately go into his "territory". This is where we are up in his face. This is where we can release all our testosterone in challenging the unbelievers, the atheists, the agnostics and all who fall the in category of the unsaved. It is where we can expend our energy and satisfy our need for action and not talk. It is where, instead of feeling useless because we can't sing, preach or teach, we can utilize our skills in carpentry, electronics, information technology, masonry, medicine and whatever field we are in to bring practical help to the saved and unsaved. Anyone who thinks that Christianity is for the weak or boring, needs to spend time on the mission field, spreading the Word of God. I could fill books just relating experiences on the mission field that challenged me and took me outside of my comfort zone. These were experiences that called upon the bravery and strength of the Lion to face the police in a particular nation for preaching the Word of God. That enabled me to face being under the constant threat of arrest and/or deportation for the gospel's sake. I learned to face being without basic amenities and medical facilities and having to rely solely upon the Lord to preserve and heal my physical body and that of the team. I could go on and on, but I believe the message is clear. Men, we have more than enough opportunities to give legitimate expression to the Lion in us while in the pursuit of Christ, without feeling that we surrendered our masculinity when we became Christians.

We need to actively stand in defense of the poor and helpless and become a voice for causes of righteousness. Men we need to strategically infiltrate and take over secular segments of influence in areas that directly impact our lives and the lives of our children. We need to become activists and not be "passivists" to coin a word. Become a part of lobby groups. Get involved in Citizen Associations, neighbourhood watches, the PTAs in your children's schools. Get involved in feeding programmes for the poor and clothes distribution. Find orphans, the fatherless and the un-fathered to father and mentor. Write articles in the newspapers expressing your Christian views and beliefs. Be on the prowl as a Lion using your strength and bravery, not to devour, but to defend, not to tear, but to mend. We should be intimidating and considered dangerous against evil and wickedness. We must boldly stand for what we believe and for right. We must challenge the culture of silence when we see wickedness and unrighteousness being committed in society and in the church.

The Leader King

Another feature of the Lion is its role as King of the jungle. God has designed man to have dominion and subdue the earth. This starts in his home. It is this desire for rulership and dominion that is in part responsible for so many church splits and plethora of churches. The kind of leadership that God is calling us to however, is that of the servant leader. Our natural leadership skills must not turn us into Dons and heads of crime syndicates, but advocates and ambassadors for the Kingdom of God, leading others to Christ. There should not be even the appearance of "donmanship" in Church fellowships or para-church organizations.

Men, as kings we need to rise up and walk in the authority that God has given to us. Too many men approach life's situations and challenges weak, powerless, already defeated. We readily give in and submit to the demands of our human bosses and the world, even to the extent of compromising our own beliefs and values, often with the excuse that we have no choice. We forget who we are and whose we are. I will never forget a lesson I learned on the mission field with my wife which has totally transformed our approach to obstacles and difficulties we might face in our daily lives as we deal with unbelievers and people in positions of "worldly power".

We were leaders of a missions team to a communist nation under military rule. I was delayed by a day but Maria went ahead of me with most of the team members, approximately eight in number. Following are excerpts of her account in her book ARISE Intercessors....Arise! (p 171-173)

> *"I was doing an annual seminar with some pastors and missionaries in a communist country. In the midst of my teaching and intercessory prayers, and while the rest of the team were with the children, the authorities arrived. They commanded us, the visiting team, to stop what we were doing and to go immediately to the nearby police station. The local pastors and other leaders however insisted on coming with us. When we arrived we were ushered inside where we all were questioned by four officials. While sitting there and listening to the interrogation being done in another language (English was not their native tongue), the Holy Spirit spoke these words to me" They are in authority but so are you!" Immediately I had a sensing that God wanted to use me and I needed to stand in my authority. Boldness came upon me. I called on our translator to interpret every word I was about to say to the communist authorities without changing or toning anything. He agreed and I stood up to speak. I did so twice and at the end of the second address, the military official suddenly told us we were free to go. As we descended the stairs, I wondered, 'Did they recognize divine authority speaking through us?'"*

After my arrival and discussing the incident with Maria, the Lord gave us an understanding that authority needs to confront authority. So when we are being confronted by those in authority, we must likewise stand in the confidence of the authority that God has given us. They are in authority but so are we. Men, don't just meekly give in. Stand up for what you want and what you believe in.

Since that time, we have seen God move on our behalf so many times to resolve situations and circumstances in our favor simply because we refuse to just take the word of, and give in to, those in worldly authority, but instead stand in the authority that we too have as royalty in God's Kingdom *(1 Pet 2:9)* and declare what we want to come to pass. Imagine how potent that authority is when exercised by the

"heirs and joints heirs with Jesus Christ" (Romans 8:17)

How the Nature of the Lamb Must Manifest In Men

The Lamb nature must always be expressed by a husband to his wife. *Ephesians 5* says: *Husbands, love your wives as Christ loves the church and gave His life for her.* Can there be any clearer example of the sacrificial nature of the Lamb being expressed here? Husbands, you need to be willing to die to your wants and your needs, for your wives. When we love our wives this way, then they will have no problem honoring, obeying and submitting to us. We need a radical change in our concept of our wives as someone there to serve us and satisfy our needs to that of them being someone so worthy and so valuable as to die for!

Fathers, the Lamb nature must for the most part be expressed by us to our children. At times, especially as they become older, the Lion might need to roar in correcting, admonishing and disciplining. However, as much as we might roar, we must never tear and devour our children. We need to be careful that the Lion in us is not beating down and discouraging our children even as we seek to guide, discipline and train them up in the way they ought to go. There is a general way that they ought to go, that is the way of the Lord, but there is also a specific way that God intends for our children to go. We need to seek God for that way specific for them and facilitate them moving in that way. Not forcing them to fulfill the dream that we had as a child but never fulfilled, to be a doctor, lawyer or businessman. Instead, we must help them to be who God wants them to be. We must heed the scriptural admonition not to provoke our children to wrath. Note this instruction was given specifically to Fathers because God knows that the Lion in us, if unleashed against our children, could destroy them.

The LAMB is naturally gentle, humble, submissive, teachable approachable and lovable. It embodies the more endearing features of our nature and balances the LION in us. As such, we should be gentle towards our loved ones, our brothers and sisters in Christ, seeking to protect and cover, not to expose and destroy.

We should be submissive to Godly leadership and those in authority, not rebellious, constantly criticizing and tearing down. We must be humble, esteeming others above ourselves.

We must be teachable, recognizing that we always can learn from others and that we do not know everything. One of the most tragic states to be in is a position of not being able to be taught. Nobody likes a "know it all", especially when it is obvious that they don't know it all, and is not willing to listen and learn. When we are not teachable, we cannot grow beyond where we are.

Biblical Examples of the Lion and the LAMB

David – Warrior (LION) and Worshipper (LAMB)

David is an excellent example of the appropriate expression of the Lion and the Lamb in a man despite his sin with Bathsheba. He was the ultimate warrior and the ultimate worshipper. He was the warrior that faced a giant twice his size, a man who was schooled in the art of war, fearsome and confident in his prowess as a soldier. However the LION in David rose up in defense of his God to declare, *"who is this uncircumcised Philistine that dare to defy the armies of the living God."* *(1 Sam 17:26)* He faced Goliath with 5 pebbles and the name of the LORD and defeated him with one stone to the forehead.

Yet he is the worshipper who danced his clothes off in worship, praise and rejoicing when the ark of the Lord was returned to Israel. He was the warrior of whom it was sung *"Saul has slain his thousands and David his tens of thousands"(1Sam18:7)* and he was the worshipper who wrote *"As the deer pants for the water so my soul longs after you"(Ps 42:1)* as well as most of the Psalms

When the enemy captured his wives and those of his soldiers, the LION in him rose up and he went and recovered them all. Yet he was the LAMB who refused to *"touch the Lord's anointed"(1Sam26:9)* in not killing Saul.

Samuel – Prophet (LION) and Priest (LAMB)

Samuel as a prophet was the one who judged Israel. He declared God's judgement upon Saul when he turned from God, but he mourned over Saul's demise. The very first prophecy that God gave Samuel was one in which the bravery of the lion had to be summoned to deliver. The prophecy was to Eli, Samuel's mentor, and how God was going to destroy every male in his family line.

I have taken the time to explain the nature and role of man as God created him so that we can understand how that nature and role needs to function in the church. It is my view that one of the greatest indictment against churches in general and the western hemisphere in particular, is the great and overwhelming imbalance in the ratio of males to females in the congregations. By observation alone I would say women generally outnumber men 3:1. I believe this is due to a lack of appreciation of the Lion and Lamb nature deposited in our men and how they ought to function and complement each other. In men, it is the Lion nature that dominates. Whereas in many cases we need to teach our men to be in touch with and release their Lamb-nature in the appropriate settings, in order to attract men to Christ and Christianity, it is to their Lion nature that we must appeal. Unfortunately, we present a very weak, passive version of Christianity that Christ and the apostles did not portray. In fact Christ himself taught the opposite when he declared in *Matt 11:12 "From the days of John the Baptist until now the kingdom of heaven suffers violence, and violent men take it by force"*. It is the Lion in us that will advance, lay hold of and possess the kingdom of God; not the Lamb.

As established previously, men are leaders, action oriented, aggressive, competitive and need to conquer and dominate. Yet we take

45

men who were all of this in their secular, sinful, unsaved lives prior to knowing Christ, and place them in the Church to be quiet, hymn-singing, passive men who just say "Hallelujah, praise the Lord", feel good and go home. Some were leaders in business, politicians, and yes even gang leaders. Yet we take the message of Christ to turn the other cheek to the extreme where we overtly and subtly teach our men that to be good Christians, they must kill the Lion in them and on all occasions become Lambs just waiting to be slaughtered. No wonder our churches are not attracting men and if they do come, they do not stay for too long. No wonder our churches are filled with mainly women. No wonder there is so much in-fighting and division in our churches and church splits as the way of settling disputes. No wonder there is so much domestic violence against wives and children among church men and church leaders. I am not condoning any of the above ills but what do we expect if we do not teach our men how to adequately and appropriately express the Lion nature within them? Many are either going to leave, start a power struggle with leadership, abuse their families at home/the weak somewhere else or all of the above.

I challenge the under-shepherds of God's people, to consider the teaching of this chapter, and prayerfully seek the Lord for the appropriate release of the Lion and Lamb in their congregations and the body of Christ. Both are essential to the church fulfilling its purpose and destiny.

Pastor Harry Walcott, President, Jamaica House Of Prayer, praying on Election Day, Feb. 25, 2016

Chapter Three

Overcoming The Concerns That Preoccupy Men and Hinder Prayer

Male identity is not essentially a matter of roles, which vary with culture and shift with changing times – it is a matter of inherent purpose.

–Myles Munroe

In an article in Christianity Today, Tanya Luhrmann/ MAY 7, 2012 pointed out that the 2008 Pew U.S. Religious Landscape Survey found that two-thirds of all the women surveyed pray daily, while less than half of all the men surveyed do. The Pew survey was unusually large, accounting for over 35,000 Americans, but gender differences in prayer frequency have been found before (notably by Paloma and Gallup in 1991).

For those who have lived with, worked with, related to men on different levels and in many spheres, taking note and paying keen attention to how they operate, these persons would have noted that men are preoccupied with similar things as women but some things weigh more heavily on the males. Not wanting to assume too much, this question was posed in some questionnaires that we sent out to men who are praying. One question that was asked was, *"What are some things that preoccupy men, which at times make prayer difficult?"* What are the joy-stealers in their lives? This is specifically addressing men who know the value of prayer but have encountered various obstacles that have not only hindered their prayers but have also **stolen the joy that comes from experiencing answers to prayers.**

The Joy-Stealers

The answers to the question were thought-provoking and insightful in helping us to understand how to encourage men generally and what issues to address in their lives specifically. The answers listed the following areas: the burden of meeting the needs of the family, being primary breadwinners; job/career; cares of life; lusts; indiscipline; social life; distractions through entertainment and busyness.

Devon:

I know that we like to do "practical" stuff and many times this gets in the way of doing something that seems impractical, but is even more practical as we seek solutions; that is, spending time in the presence of the Creator of the universe, the Omnipotent, Omniscient One, and avail ourselves of His wisdom, strength and guidance through praying.

Here are some hindrances that were shared by several men in prayer:

o **Indiscipline**: Being disciplined enough to reserve time to pray is a problem for many men. The word indiscipline means unruliness, rowdiness, disorderliness, insubordination, disruptive behavior. Since a part of our nature is that we like to rule and control, we have to watch out for the down-side of this characteristic. We can allow things to get out of hand that we should be keeping under control. Our prayer life is one such thing. It seems easier to try to control people than our own bodies and minds. *Prov 16:32 (KJV)* states that *"He that ruleth his spirit is better than he that taketh a city"*

Men, we need to ensure that we are ruling our spirits and exercising self-control. Many men after conquering the corporate world, excelling in sports, living the "successful" life, find themselves undone by their lack of discipline and self-control.

2 Timothy1:7 (KJV) says:
For God hath not given us the spirit of fear; but of power, and of love, and of a **sound mind**.

The word translated "sound mind" is better translated in other versions as ***self-control***. As we wrestle with indiscipline, let us remember and hold on to the truth that God has given us a spirit of self-control.

o **Busyness**: The daily grind of work, making financial provisions, the various roles one plays – husband, father, manager or worker, and working long hours to meet financial needs can be a hindrance to setting aside time to pray. For some of us, we would wish that things could slow down; go back to the simple life when we were not so rushed, pushed and stretched beyond our time-limits. The reality that faces us is that it is getting worse. Technology has made life easier in some ways – we can now connect with the world through the worldwide web, however, we now have the world in our "space" all the time and that is a lot to deal with. God knew that this time would come and I believe that He went ahead and made provisions for this crunch period and season that seems never ending.

One fundamental truth that Maria and I have come to understand and appreciate about people and men especially, is that we find time to do what we want to do. The bottom line is that if we think something is important enough, or want something badly enough, we will make time for it. This is especially apparent in the area of our pursuit of wealth and the opposite sex. I have rarely heard men say that they are too busy when being presented with a money-making idea or when trying to win the affection of someone of the fairer sex. We will go to extremes, as the poets say, cross the widest ocean, climb the highest mountain, spend hours, days, weeks, months to win the heart and affection of our "princess".

Men, we spend time to pursue our passions, be it in sports, hobbies or entertainment, so let us not use the excuse that we are too busy to spend time in the presence of God. If we are to be honest with ourselves, the real issue is that spending time with God is not important enough to us neither do we want it badly enough! We need to change our mindsets so that this becomes a top priority and a passion for us. Spending time with God is just like with the opposite sex. The more time we spend with Him, the better we get to know Him and understand Him, which creates a desire to spend even more time with Him.

o **Unmet Needs**: Other areas of a man's life where he feels his needs are not being met can be an area of constant distraction by occupying his thoughts and motivating actions. Prominent areas include the ***need for sex and recognition or respect among colleagues***. Our jobs are a major area of our productivity and our intimate relationships, another. If we don't feel like we are producing in any of these areas, then we are seriously put out. What better place to go to deal with the void of lack of productivity than to talk honestly with our Heavenly Father and to ask Him to act expeditiously on our behalf. What better time to go to him than when we are feeling sexually frustrated and having to resist the temptation of the "skirts" in our faces on the streets and in the media. He awaits us coming to Him as sons!

o **Lacking Creativity**: Being able to develop a pragmatic approach that does not necessarily require a "special" place but rather praying as one goes about one's affairs and as one faces various circumstances would allow for spontaneity in prayer. Prayer then becomes a lifestyle and not an event; a "pragmatic approach" which is typical of the male specie. Men will look for practical and realistic solutions when faced with a dilemma. It has to be a *pray-I-must* attitude. Therefore, if I have to do it as I go, it just has to be done. I will pray in my car, at the bus-stop, while driving in public transportation, in the men's room, while mowing the yard, checking under the bonnet of the vehicle, waiting in a restaurant, waiting on the match to start and yes, even while the match is on, God shows me things to pray for.

o **Entertainment:** Too much time is spent on TV, sports, news and on the internet. *"Guilty as charged"* I can hear most men responding. As humans, we like to be entertained and this is the reason Hollywood and the media corporations have prospered. We will pay, even a high price, to be entertained. For some, the rent can wait to be paid but the cable has to stay on! It is interesting to note however, from years watching the fallout of an increasing appetite for entertainment that men have weakened considerably in their walk with God; men have fallen increasingly into immorality; men have increasingly deserted their families and the Church. One has to wonder if there is not a correlation between the aforementioned and the easy accessibility of demonic lures through entertainment right in our bedrooms, pockets, and waistbands that come just at the click of a button! What has God been saying to us especially as Christian men? If we were to put entertainment on one side of the scale and our love of God demonstrated through the amount of time we spend relating to Him, on the other side of the scale, which side would be lighter?

Maria:

o **Various Lusts**: Men have confessed to me that they have pulled back from ministering in the Church, whether by rejecting the invitation to do so or by giving up ministry posts, because they have felt that they are unable to control their lustful appetites. I would want to point out here that all of these lustful cravings have not been only in the area of illicit sexual gratification but lust for power, position and material possessions. Men seem to withdraw more easily when they feel slighted when bringing their thoughts and solutions into a situation; overlooked for promotion or remuneration; unrecognized for the value they bring to the relationship, home, organization or community. The hardest thing for men is to just "suck it up" and keep moving. Yet, Jesus is the primary example here.

(a) As a man Jesus was tempted in the same way as men are, yet without sinning *(Hebrews 4:15)*. Jesus was a full-blooded man as He was also divine. He got hungry, tired, sleepy and I am sure He had hormones kicking inside as He developed into a man and had natural attraction towards women. The Bible in no way indicates otherwise.

(b) Jesus made Himself of no reputation - *Phill 2:7*. I know that this does not sound good to the carnal nature but if Christian men are going to win the battle in an unfair, unjust and lop-sided world, they have to be willing to put down the desire for "reputation"! Reputation has to do with standing, status, making a name for oneself; how one sees you at work, play or in fellowship. If you should lose status at any point with man, it does not mean that you have lost status with God. As a matter of fact, sometimes a Christian may have to lose that status in men's eyes in order to gain status with God

Help...Help...Help!

How then can men be helped with dealing with these issues, especially when they are living in a context where there is increasing job-losses, keeping up with the fast-paced changes in the global economy, having to find multiple streams of income in order to ensure the quality of life that they desire for their family; having an increasing appetite for pleasure of all types? Help is needed because these factors do not seem to allow time for spending the quantity and quality time that men need to develop in their personal walk with God, and to find the grace and strength to lead in the various roles in their lives. Yet, it is for this very reason and seemingly insurmountable hurdle why men **have to** find time to pray! If not, they will find themselves battling mental, emotional and physical challenges that are usually stress-related illnesses but could have been avoided if they found time to spend with the Prince of Peace. He would ensure that on a daily basis, they would have *"peace which passes all understanding"*. *(Phil. 4:7)*

In my decades of formally and informally counselling with men, I have found that finances, sex and a general need to be respected and appreciated in the home and workplace have been serious hindrances in their Christian walk and subsequently their devotional life. Much of the backsliding among the male specie, from my discourse with men who once walked with God, came from not knowing how to rein in their appetites! The area of sexual immorality has been the primary fiend. Dr. Myles Munroe in his book, *Understanding the Purpose and Power of Men,* in attempting to help men to understand the role sex should play in their lives points out that *"God established marriage so the sexual relationship can be full of pleasure—not repercussions and remorse." (p 170)* I have counselled men who are full of guilt and packed with remorse but I have also been sadly struck by those who are beyond remorse. It is as if their consciences are *"seared with a hot iron"*, as the Scripture puts it in *1 Timothy 4:2.* These men have lost their love for God; love for family and lost a general sense of values. They had moved outside of God's protective boundaries and limitations for sex and were now on a slippery road to reprobation. It is heart-breaking to see what the Enemy has done to males made in God's image and likeness because

Men seem to withdraw more easily when they feel slighted when bringing their thoughts and solutions into a situation; overlooked for promotion or remuneration; unrecognized for the value they bring to the relationship, home, organization or community.

they have moved from under God's loving Fatherly covering!

This section is not a note for judgement or condemnation of God's sons who struggle in this manner. This is a means to encourage men who struggle in this way and who have "suffered" through having an anemic prayer life, as a result, to use the very medium of prayer, if possible, by getting together with other men to pray concerning these areas that the Enemy has used throughout the centuries to keep many men spiritually impoverished. It is time for breakthrough! Men of God, I stand with you today to declare what the Scripture says of you, " ...*I have written unto you, young men, because ye are strong, and the word of God abideth in you, and ye have overcome the wicked one.*" (1 John 2:13, KJV)

Is Distraction Hindering Men From Listening to God?

Devon:

Answers to prayers come many times in hearing God speak to us – Yes, No, Not Now. Most times this "hearing God" requires time and patience in listening for His answers. If we are perpetually distracted, it is more difficult and for some, even impossible to listen. Sometimes we might not want to listen because we are pre-empting or wanting to forget the outcome! Some men just simply think that God takes too long to act. They cannot sit around and wait. They are pragmatic in nature and feel they have to do something, and do it now. We had some feedback as we posed the issue to some praying men. We asked them if they found it difficult to listen to God when they pray – listening afterwards for His instructions? We believe you will find the responses informative, instructive and certainly, beneficial.

I sometimes do (get distracted), due to the pressure of time, but the part I actually enjoy most about my prayer life is hearing from God. There is an excitement, a thrill to know that I have heard from, and been in communication with the King of the universe. Not just a monologue of me doing all the talking, but a true dialogue; Him talking back to me. To deal with the time pressure, I have to remind myself that this is the most important thing that I will be doing for the day- conversing with my King. I also remind myself, as I have often seen, that this time spent with Him, on many occasions ends up saving me so much time during the day, as He orders my step and saves me from mis-steps that would have cost me time. I must confess though, that I do get **disappointed** when I don't hear from Him for days or longer, which does happen. This disappointment many times has led to discouragement in being consistent especially in praying over particular matters relating to areas of struggles and temptation.

My wife usually picks this up and encourages me to stand firm in prayer. One of the things I have come to appreciate over the years of waiting on God is that our obedience or lack thereof does affect God's response to us. The truth is, God is not obligated to respond to us if we have not yet obeyed Him in the last thing He has said to us. If He has given us specific instructions or advice that we are not following, why should He continue to speak to us until we have obeyed? Don't we do the same with our children? How many times have they come to us and we say to them that we are still waiting on them to do what we have instructed or to heed the advice we have given, and until they do we have nothing further to say? So when I find myself in that spot where God seems to be silent, I ask myself, "Have I obeyed or heeded His last instruction or advice? It is possible you might need to do the same.

Some praying men listen to get a sense from God of how to approach a particular petition and to see whether or not they should make the request at all. One intercessor said: "While I'm praying, I like to listen so I'm continually guided by His Spirit. When I'm done praying there is the habit of quickly moving on to the next task since it's not often that I hear additional instructions from God." What is impressive is the fact that he waits for directions not just after he prays but before he prayed to know how and what to pray. Isn't this in keeping with the Scriptures in *Romans 8:26(KJV)*, which says, *"We do not know what we ought to pray"*. Listening during the time of praying is also critical since we know that many times we go to God with a written or unwritten prayer list and if we allow the Holy Spirit to take over, we may leave the prayer "closet" not even mentioning what was consuming our thoughts when we entered.

About half of the men in prayer we asked admitted to having a struggle in this area if not all the time, at least sometimes. Some pointed out that, "It is a learnt discipline to listen". They are often rushed or pressed for time and therefore don't wait to listen. Admittedly however, it was recognized among the men that they should. The truth is, as put by a praying pastor, "It is worth nothing though, if many times we are too busy and though we pray, we do not spend enough time to listen or find time to stay patiently with God to hear His instructions."

It seems to me that the world is moving at an increasingly faster pace. If the discipline is not developed now, to wait patiently and listen to God in prayer, it will become progressively harder. The workplaces are demanding more, sometimes even wanting the men to work on their day of worship although they are not working in essential services. The family is also demanding more. Gone are the days when men and women have clearly defined roles. While women are joining in being "providers", men are joining in being "nurturers" within the family. Going to work and then returning home to nurture is not easy for either genders, but this is the very reason, the demands of this duality of roles, why we need to draw on God's strength, His grace and His Fatherly guidance, in prayer. Men, you can do it! Although multi-tasking might not be your main strength, if there is one thing I know that God is committed to doing for you, and that is, helping you to find Him and having found Him, to remain faithful.

Are Men Convinced That Prayer Works?

Maria:

I wanted to get to the heart of the men concerning matters of prayer. One of the questions I needed to be answered was: "Are men convinced that prayer works?" I deliberately asked male intercessors, intercessory leaders or interceding Ministers of Religion serving within and beyond my nation. The deeper question was, "What has made them hold out in praying faithfully over decades?" All of the answers, no matter how they were stated, had one kernel in the answer – the results - the answered prayer! Men are truly results-oriented and this is the reason why their minds hasten to find a solution to a problem and they do not necessarily want to talk a lot about it or sit around attempting to dissect it.

To me nothing is a greater evidence of the efficacy of prayer than the greater intimacy and faith that develops between men and God. As much as we are results oriented, let us pursue that intimacy with God, to know Him face -to - face!

So the males whose brains we picked, all agreed that they were motivated to pray by the results they achieved when they prayed. Here are some of the responses to the question, "In your own life, what convinced you that prayer works/is effective?":

- o The results derived from praying (a Worship Leader)
- o The testimonies of answered prayers (a Pastor and Journalist)
- o Manifest results- healing, provision, circumstances. Personal experience – peace rest, assurance, hope. (a Pastor and Agriculturalist)
- o Seeing the efficacy of prayer at work through my mother, other believers, through my readings, teachings received and my own experiences. (a Pastor and Lawyer)
- o I have seen evidence of answers to my prayers time and time again. (Pastor and Telecommunications worker)
- o Testimonies (Canadian)
- o I have seen answers to prayer in a very short time after the request was made. Answers to prayer that came a very long time after the request, has also built my faith and encouraged me to be more persistent in prayer. (Intercessor and Sound technician)

o I have seen answers to prayer but more importantly praying builds relationship with God. It is a joy to pray and hear God. (Minister, Telecommunications Engineer)

What is it that convinces a man that prayer works? It is what he sees resulting from investing his time in praying. We could then ask the question: Are men likely to be turned off from praying if they are not seeing results, in other words not experiencing answers to their prayers? If we are to help men to pray more, should our prayers be appealing to God to manifest Himself more to them in tangible answers to their prayers, especially in areas that affect men more than women. This subject will be dealt with in subsequent chapters.

One point that I want men to take particular note of, is that a critical aspect of knowing that prayer works, apart from the results of prayer and answers to prayer, is the relationship that is built and strengthened between ourselves and God. To us, nothing is a grander evidence of the efficacy of prayer than the greater intimacy and faith that develops between men and God. As much as we are results oriented, let us pursue that intimacy with God, to know Him face-to-face!

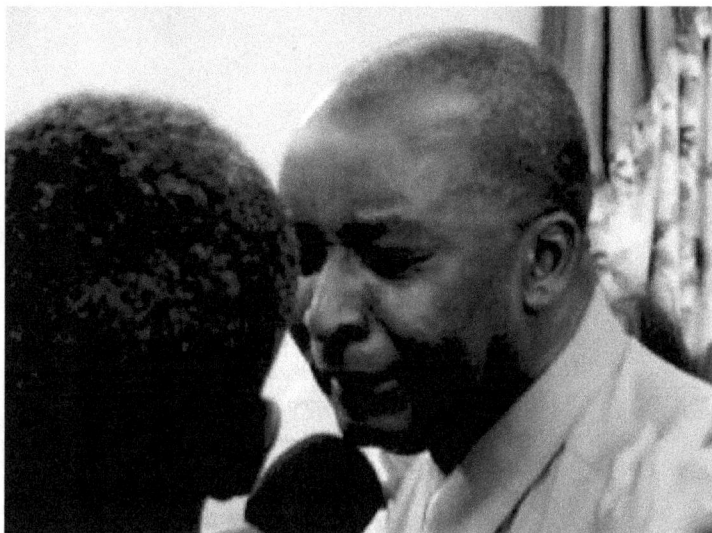

Rev. Naila Ricketts, President of Prayer 2000, praying at the Caribbean Prayer Summit, Jamaica

Chapter Four

Dealing with Men's Turn-Off From Prayer in the Church

Men mistakenly expect women to think, communicate, and react the way men do; women mistakenly expect men to feel, communicate, and respond the way women do.

--John Gray

We tend to move towards the things that attract us but to move away from what repels us. This was the thought behind this question, is there anything within the Church that turns men off from prayer and cause them not to want to participate, hence stifling and diluting their potency in prayer? If many men are not showing up in our prayer meetings, apart from their general internal and other distractions discussed in previous chapters, are there some modus operandi in our Church fellowships and prayer meetings that repel men? Could there be some practices that our Churches may need to look at? Are there aspects of the behaviour of women, probably men too, in prayer contexts, that might be a temptation to men to mentally, if not physically, "check out" (tune out their thoughts and emotions) while praying is taking place? Do some men just plainly do not want to associate with our prayer meetings?

A few of the brethren with which we discussed this could not think of anything that would turn them off from praying, wherever. That was comforting. However, there were others who admitted to being turned off at times and willingly expressed the reasons for this.

Devon:

I know it is natural to express emotions in prayer, but whenever I detect those feelings or emotions are phony and for effect or to seem to be spiritual, this is a turn off for me. Let's look at some other areas of "turn-off" shared, followed by how we can address these turn-offs:

Emotionalism: Some men are turned off by the "emotional" aspect. One male retorted: "It often times is all emotional and seldom feels like a conversation with God. Sometimes it feels like something we are supposed to do rather than a connection between two individuals." The viewpoint of those holding such a stance is that, prayer is "more about a conversation and less about the emotion". Though the point is taken, I (Devon) have never heard a conversation without emotion. Two people engaged in conversation are always expressing emotions which will vary of course based on the topic, passion and personality of the participants. Conversations without emotions are usually monologues or lectures, and even then emotion may be expressed. The point being made is that emotions should not seem extreme in public praying but that such intercession is best expressed in one's personal prayer closet. Emotionalism is usually ascribed to women who many males believe make decisions and react more out of emotions than a rational and practical approach to life. Their prayers may even be judged with this background notion. Gentlemen, if this notion was a fact, you would need to address why, many times, women have also been correct when giving advice or suggestions based on **intuition**. This is a kind of insight and sensitivity that God placed in this gender that have helped to steer men away from danger and blindness to consequences. *(I Sam 25:23-33; Judges 4:4-10)*. God even chose to speak to them and not their husbands initially. Could that have something to do with the fact that they don't filter everything through their minds as we men practice doing? Have our minds and mindset often gotten in the way of our faith, a necessary ingredient to approach God and to receive answers to prayers?

Ritualistic Monotony: The sense of randomness, sameness, and ritualistic monotony of prayer was a turn-off.

Maria:

I thought to myself that this might very well be as a result of lack of teaching. I wondered if the disciples were having this sensing even within themselves when they asked Jesus to teach them to pray. (Luke 11:4) Many men believe that prayer should be engaging. One male pastor shared: "Where there is ritualistic monotony and inattentiveness to engage, I am turned off." Another intercessor saw this monotony in what he termed, "prescribed/standardized topics", that is in relation to prayer.

So the question that one could ask is this: Could men be generally bored with the way we conduct prayer in our Churches/prayer meetings? Before there is an outcry of defense to this question, we could ask another. Are there men who God is waiting on, whose hearts will be sold out to passionately go after Him, even in prayer? Men who could wake up the Church to other dimensions of prayer that, because it is effectual and fervent, it brings results. (Jas 5:16)? Could you be that man?

Escapism: To some men, it seems that prayer is used as an escapist route from personal responsibility, thus a lack of a proper appreciation of its utility as an act of worship. This is an interesting note since from my seminary days we were reading of those who taught that Christianity was the "opium of the masses" – some sort of escape route from reality. We need to note this observation since prayer should not be seen as a denial or distraction where God expects us to act and do what we know we ought to do in a given situation. I would use for example a scenario where we are asking God whether or not we should love someone who is being unkind to us. This would seem like wasted prayer since we already know the Scriptural command is to love, even our enemies. Our personal responsibility is to act on God's Word and not to sit around praying the obvious. Our true worship, before God, even in praying, is to do what He commands us to do. When we are finished singing our songs, clapping our hands, stomping our feet and praying, we still have the responsibility to obey God's instructions!

Cacophony in Praying: When everyone prays aloud at the same time, some men are turned off. When there seems to be the sound of "discord" or "disharmony" in prayer, it becomes a distraction to praying. Church culture seems to be what dictates this. There is one culture that believes strongly in the "agreement" in praying and therefore would deem it necessary for persons to pray one-at-a-time so that the prayers can be heard and agreed with. They use the Scripture, "If two of you shall agree" (Matt. 18:19) as their basis for allowing one person to pray while the others listen and come into agreement. There is the other side of the fence, however, who believe that God is not confused or distracted and can hear us pray all at once! They believe that they are lifting their voices to God in one accord. The question is, is there a place in the Church for both? Would men like these who are turned off by the lack of symphony, not have an issue if they were allowed to hear what is being prayed the majority of the times so that they can know whether to say "Amen" or "Not so Lord Jesus"?

Limited Male Involvement: Low number participation, reluctance to engage in prayer among males and limited male involvement was a serious turn off for one male pastor. It is said that men attract other men to be involved in certain types of activities and men will listen only to other men when being taught particular life-skills. If this statement is a fact then one can understand that if men, especially the younger generation, do not see their male predecessors stepping up to the plate when prayer meetings are called and generally fully participating in praying, they could easily, even subconsciously believe that prayer is more for women. Again, this is not what is seen in the Scriptures. Those who engaged God in prayer were strong men, leading men, family men, prophetic men, men sold-out to God!

No Manifested Power: The demonstration of the power gifts was an attraction for some to prayer meetings. One seasoned male intercessor pointed out that he is drawn when "there is a manifestation of God's Spirit through, prophecy, deliverance, healing, etc. I am discouraged from participating in prayer gatherings where participants are satisfied with making petitions to God void of His manifest presence." Wow! I wondered if he would want to be praying in our

64

average Churches. How many men actually think like him? As a man of prayer is he unique in his longing?

There is an increased longing and a cry generally for God's manifested presence and power in His Church and in our lives today. There might be men with this longing specifically in the place of prayer where they want to see results. Their motivation for attending prayer meetings might be an assurance that others who pray with them will not settle for monotony but for manifestation. These are men who will put God to the test, in a Scriptural way. They want to "prove Him" and challenge what they see of Him in His Word. Perhaps pretty much like Moses and others did when they were in conflict and confusion, being faced with their enemies on all sides and when they were challenged with stepping out into the deep. What then should be done to engage men to participate in prayer meetings and generally in praying in the Church? As we continue to learn more about what praying men think about prayer, we will be able to surmise not just from their valuable opinions but from what the Holy Spirit would want to teach men of God about prayer.

How To Engage Men's Participation

What then should be done to engage men to participate in prayer meetings and generally in praying in the Church? We would like to offer some suggestions in summarizing the responses received as well as from our own experiences from leading both sexes in the prayer movement.

➤ **The Lion Must Roar**. One website addressed this issue in an article, *A way to encourage men to pray*, and made the following suggestion: "I think we could and should appeal to the warrior God has put inside men." [http://cuyahogavalleychurch.blogspot.com].This reminds me of Devon's Lion and the Lamb message shared in Chapter 2. I have watched over the years, men being impacted generally and specifically in their prayer lives as he shares about the "Lion" in them that needs to roar at the right time. This would help the

Church not to unintentionally "feminize" men and their responses in prayer. The article also encouraged men in this way:

You are in a war, men and young men. You have an enemy. His name is the devil, Lucifer, Satan. He wants to steal, kill and destroy everything good in your life. And prayer is your number one weapon. The Christian army advances on its knees. But many of you are fighting this fight with a pop gun.

Don't blow me off, men. I don't care if you're a middle linebacker type. I don't care if you make $250,000 a year. I don't care how many people work for you. If you don't pray, you're a spiritual wimp. And the day will come when you will regret your spiritual passivity.

God is waiting. He's waiting on you to pray. You need to say, "I can and I will prevail in prayer – for my wife, my children, my grandchildren, my church, my business, my world."

It's time to man up, men. And start on your knees. If you don't pray for your family, your career, your future, who will?

➤ **The Holy Spirit and Personal Passion Must Accompany Our Praying**. How do we help the Church to get rid of monotonous praying? One of the things that drive men is passion and another is a need to conquer. Usually if there is nothing to conquer and no passion to motivate them then things become dull and like a wheel that needs to be properly oiled for effective movement. I would like to suggest to men of God that you need to have what drove the Apostles and even persons like David. It was the "oil" of the presence of the Holy Spirit in their lives. The Holy Spirit causes the roar of the Lion of the Tribe of

Judah to come out of you. The Holy Spirit brings forth a type of dynamism in prayer that moves us beyond the ritual and formula-based, every-time-we-have-to-do-it-this-way approach to prayer.

There was something that drove David into the presence of the Lord whether privately or corporately, and it's the same thing that I have seen motivating men who have cultivated a serious prayer life. This motivating factor is a panting after God, like an animal or human would after water, if they have been thirsty for a long time. Psalm 42:1, David exclaims, "As the deer pants for the water brooks, So pants my soul for You, O God." (NKJV) The men who have been with us in our Prayer ministry have been passionately pursuing God. They have, in spite of weaknesses and challenges, sought to bring down "Goliaths" in the nation, in their families and in their personal lives. I believe that this life and walk in the Spirit have truly kept them faithful on the mountain of prayer.

➢   **Extreme Form Of Emotionalism Or Rationalism Can Be A Detractor To Prayer.** Not everything that is laid out in the Scriptures makes sense to the mind. Our emotions however must be balanced by the Holy Spirit. Although it would be difficult to express passion without emotion, emotion must not be mistaken for passion. Emotions tend to be circumstantial – based on how I am feeling now in a given situation or on a given day. Passion, however, drives us even when we might not want to "feel" anything. It would be similar to Jeremiah not wanting to speak the word of the Lord because the consequences were unpleasant. However, his passion which came out of His calling, made him have the sensation of "fire shut up" within him. (Jeremiah 20:9) He became weary from holding it in. May God cause His men to become weary of shutting up their prayers and motivate them with a passion to pray.

➢   **Is There A Cause**? One of the things that motivate men in general is action. Men are more doers than talkers. Men have risen up and brought down even kingdoms and nations because they were sold out to a cause. They were convinced that there was the need for action to be taken. Each man of God has to answer this question for himself, honestly. Is there a cause for men to be involved in and leading prayer? Would certain things change – the kingdom of darkness be brought down – if men would rise up and pray?

> There was something that drove David into the presence of the Lord whether privately or corporately, and it's the same thing that I have seen motivating men who have cultivated a serious prayer life. This motivating factor is a panting after God, like an animal or human would after water, if they have been thirsty for a long time.

I have seen drastic changes made in this nation and can remember specific prayers offered up by a man on one issue. One example is hearing a Bishop stand in governmental intercession decreeing that particular artistes who were corrupting our young people with their music be stopped now. Not long after that prayer, the main cohort leader was arrested and convicted on murder charges. That brought a type of "silence" in that arena that seemed to have been impossible prior to that happening. I also witnessed a male intercessor, while prayer walking a volatile community, lift up both hands to the heavens while walking across an open area that was called, "NO MAN'S LAND". Neither side in that community dared to cross it. Yet this man of God, walked across it declaring that it was God's land and the violence would stop. He seemed like the lone David going out to meet Goliath! It was not very long after this prayer walk that I heard an announcement on the radio of an international team coming to do a Crusade and the venue was...you guessed it, No Man's Land.

I was asked to do intercessory prayer at that Crusade and Psalm 51, the repentance psalm was what God led me to pray for the Church, that community and the nation. I still remember, although it was over a decade ago, an unusual anointing that shook me from head to toe as I led the congregation, which were thousands of people on No Man's Land in prayer. I believe that what this man of God did, is what God wants many of his men to do. Go out into the field and dare to trod where no man wants to risk his life to go and declare who is Boss in that area. This male intercessor refused to take no for an answer.

Another event brought us prayer walking into a volatile area in Western Kingston, Jamaica. As we walked, a few persons from the community were bold enough to join us. As we were leading the walk we noticed a deserted looking community, and it was confirmed by the residents that no one was living there. It was void of even animals. The people were fearful to cross over into its borders, but we were led of the Lord to cross it. Mingling with us, the residents took on a brave heart. With the men at my side, we crossed it. We approached a large piece of zinc in the road. One resident came up to me and informed us that this was where criminals dumped dead bodies of persons they murdered. One visiting male minister, Pastor Daniel Perez, who on his short visit to Jamaica decided to join us, fell on his knees at the edge of the piece of zinc and began to cry out to God for forgiveness and mercy! Other men and I followed suit. We repented before God for the innocent blood that was shed in that place before continuing our walk. We continued down that street and up the other major street of the community. The place was desolate. It was true. Not one animal was to be seen and certainly no humans.

A few months after, we returned to prayer- walk that same area. The residents who came on the previous walk told us that persons had begun to move into the before deserted houses. As we walked, we sang our praises and gave God the glory as we saw a few houses occupied, persons moving around and fixing up their homes, women putting up curtains at their windows, etc. What a God we serve! I will never forget Daniel Perez's bold action and his strong prayers along with the other men that day. I was emboldened to walk that community because, apart from the presence of a Mighty God, there was the presence of brave praying men. Yes, there is something about leading an army into battle, as a woman, and having the male watchmen surrounding you in battle! There is a level of protection that is felt that is completely different from when we are surrounded by women. Don't get me wrong. God will use the women in the absence of the men but I believe that there are many occasions when God would have wanted the men to provide even physical protection but they were missing in action!

➢ **Pastors Leading By Example**. In an article titled, *Pastors' Strategies for Mobilizing Men to Pray*, the author writes:

> *In every war, warriors need generals who sound the battle call clearly and loudly. Spiritual warfare is no different. Men must be summoned to the fight by a visionary leader, and that leader should be their pastor.*

> *If men are going to effectively fight on their knees, they will need pastors who take spiritual warfare and strategic prayer personally and seriously. Victory requires a new breed of shepherd–one who leads the way into the arena of prayer.*

[Phil Miglioratti, http://www.churchleaders.com]

70

In a Church, prayer must never be relegated to a Prayer Leader while the shepherd absences him/herself from the prayer meetings. This is even more crucial with a male pastor leading men. Men do follow men. Men like to labour beside other men. It is easier for the typical male to take instructions from other males. When the males in a fellowship notice that their male shepherd does not attend prayer meetings, the message they get, irrespective of instructions issued from the platform by that leader for them to show up at prayer meetings, is that prayer is optional for men. Another message that could be received by them is that prayer is really for the women.

Phil Miglioratti gives a few suggestions that would be relevant to our discussion. He postulates that *"Pastors must reclaim their role as one who leads the troops into battle (see Joshua 5:13-6:27)."* Gone are the days when pastors lead only devotionally and outline a few scriptures meditationally. Gone are the days when the talk from the pulpit is only about consecration because after we have consecrated ourselves, we walk out those doors to face a live Enemy who we must wrestle against. *(Ephesians 6:10-12)* The pastor must understand spiritual warfare himself and be able to lead the congregation, from the front, in full engagement, into the battles of life. Miglioratti writes:

> *For men to fight on their knees, they will require more than a battle call; they must have a battle cry. They must grasp the reason, pulsate with the passion, and embrace the vision. A battle cry is loud, not simply to catch everyone's attention, but to express deep desire and desperation. A pastor who wants to lead his men into battle must have a cry, a burden; he cannot simply make an announcement.*

[[Phil Miglioratti, http://www.churchleaders.com]

As was pointed out before, there is a cause and God's men must not only recognize that cause but want to jump into action and do something about the problem – something that men are naturally wired to do. Bring solutions to a problem!

The picture that comes to mind very quickly when thinking about a male pastor who models for the men, walking the walk through spiritual warfare, is King David. David had 600 fighting men who were not the elite of his society. They were not even at all times rational thinkers, especially when their own stuff got touched by the Enemy. *(I Samuel 30)* They however stuck with him and even after he became a king, for the tenure of his rule, they were mentioned – faithful, loyal, battle-winning men of war. The last chapter of David's life pointed to the feats of his mighty men *(II Sam 23:8-38)* I wonder what was it about David, a worshipper, a man of prayer and a warrior-king that engaged the loyalty of these men?

King David was a Model and a Motivational Leader. The men who followed him did so because he led by example and he was anointed by God. The anointing is attractive to people. If men can learn from their warrior-pastor and get even some of the anointing that is upon him, many will feel that they are good to go. If men can observe their male pastors and see them maneuver their way successfully through life's challenges and personal struggles, they will want to follow. When men see their pastor's stand in faith to the point of risking their lives for the cause of Christ, men will have no excuse not to follow. When men see the Spirit of the Lord rest upon their Shepherd in a similar way that He came upon David and upon Jesus, men will stand in awe of their God and be challenged to follow.

Men, what if your pastor is a female or what if your pastor is not that model at all? You still have a model, and this model is Christ. You can press into God for yourself and be raised up as a captain and even a general in His Body. You may be the one to motivate the men around you in your fellowship and lead them into battle against your common Enemy.

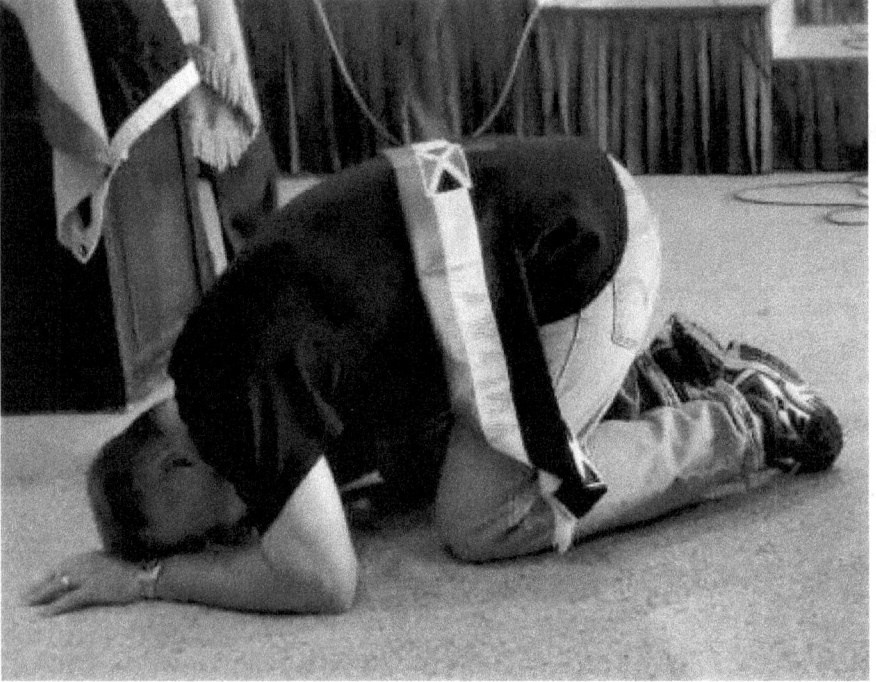

Quintin Wright, missionary to Jamaica with Jamaica House Of Prayer, praying at the National Intercessory Prayer Network of Jamaica's "Clarion Call Meeting", 2016

Chapter Five

The Cave vs. The Closet

*And he came thither unto a cave, and
lodged there; and, behold, the word of
the LORD came to him, and he said unto
him, What doest thou here, Elijah?
(1Kings 19:9- KJV)*

Devon:

I have always been fascinated by the account of the life of Elijah
as recorded in the book of 1 Kings. He is considered to be one of the
greatest Old Testament prophets that ever lived. Certain prophecies
regarding the coming of the Messiah appeared to be contingent on his
return, which was fulfilled through John the Baptist, as attested to by
Jesus Christ himself, who said of John in *Matt 11:14(NKJV)* *"And if
you are willing to receive it, he is Elijah who is to come."* Yet the main
story of Elijah's ministry is recorded in merely 6 chapters of the Bible, 1
Kings 17-19, 21 and 2 Kings 1-2. Elijah appeared out of nowhere,
without fanfare, introduction or ancestry, no claim to fame, an unknown
who burst on the scene with the words *"Now Elijah the Tishbite from
Tishbe" (I Kings 17:1)*. One would think that the greatest Old Testament
prophet would have gotten a better introduction than that, but he did not.

However, in just two chapters and the space of three years,
Elijah had bound up the clouds so they could not produce rain until he
said so, had birds providing his meals, caused a handful of flour and a
little oil to miraculously replenish themselves whenever they were used,
raised a dead boy to life, single-handedly took on the prophets of Baal
and proved Jehovah to be the one true God by sending down fire from
heaven to consume the sacrifice, destroyed the prophets of Baal, brought
an end to the drought and outran a team of chariot horses *(I Kings 17-
18)*.

Then comes, in my opinion one of the most surprising and baffling turn of events recorded in scripture. After such a miracle filled, power packed ministry described above and coming right after victory in one of the greatest challenges ever recorded, one man against 850 false prophets, we read in *1 Kings 19:2-3*:

> *2Then Jezebel sent a messenger unto Elijah, saying, So let the gods do to me, and more also, if I make not thy life as the life of one of them by tomorrow about this time. 3And when he saw (heard) that, he arose, and went (fled) for his life...*

Yes men, this mighty prophet who took on all challengers became afraid and fled at the threat of one woman. No matter how strong and powerful we feel at times, no matter how mightily God might have used us, is using us, will use us, we can and do get afraid. But guess what, it is ok, to be afraid. I know he has called us to be strong and courageous *(Joshua 1:6)*, but strength and courage does not mean lack of fear, on the contrary it means the ability to face and conquer our fears. We do not need strength and courage to face what we do not fear. Being afraid is ok. When the bible tells us to "Fear not", it is simply telling us to not let our fears paralyze or deter us and cause us to miss out on what God wants to do in our lives. Yes, being afraid is not indicative of failure, how we deal with our fears is what determines whether we fail or succeed.

In this instance, Elijah allowed his fear to overcome him and succumbing to despair, he fled to a cave of hiding, a place God never sent him. Listen to God's question in *1 Kings 19:9 "And he came thither unto a cave, and lodged there; and, behold, the word of the LORD came to him, and he said unto him, What doest thou here, Elijah?"* God did not send Elijah to that cave, he was driven there by his fear.

In His best-selling book, *Men are from Mars, Women are from Venus,* John Gray examines the differences between men and women especially in the area of communication and relationships. He likens these differences to that of persons coming from different planets, the men from Mars and the women from Venus. Chapter 3 of his book is entitled "Men goes to their caves, Women talk". In this chapter Gray states:

> *"When a Martian gets upset he never talks about what is bothering him. He would never burden another Martian with his problem unless his friend's assistance was necessary to solve the problem. Instead he becomes very quiet and goes to his private cave to think about his problem, mulling it over to find a solution. When he has found a solution, he feels much better and comes out of his cave"* (John Gray, Men are From Mars, Women are from Venus, p 13).

Both men and women can identify with this aspect of male behaviour. It is indeed very typical for males to withdraw into their caves, into themselves, to deal with their issues. However, for the Christian male I would like to suggest that instead of withdrawing into our caves, we run into our "closets", our prayer closets, which could even be a literal space where you will often go to be alone with God. Many of the patriarchs, prophets and even Jesus did this.

When the bible tells us to "Fear not", it is simply telling us to not let our fears paralyze or deter us and cause us to miss out on what God wants to do in our lives. Yes, being afraid is not indicative of failure, how we deal with our fears is what determines whether we fail or succeed.

Moses was often seen going off in the mountains, to commune with God *(Exod19:3, 20; 24:15-18)*. Jacob had life-changing experiences while meeting alone with God *(Gen 32:9-13, 22-32)*. Daniel, while in Babylon, *(Dan. 6:10; 9:1-19)* would withdraw to his room, turn his face towards Jerusalem and commune with his God. He did this so often that it was the only way that his enemies could entrap him and accuse him before the king *(Dan 6:11-16)*. Nehemiah did so when he needed a solution and intervention when the walls of Jerusalem were broken down and when he was constantly being harassed by his enemies who wanted him to stop building *(Neh. 1:4-11; 6:9, 14)*.

When Elijah ran into the wilderness and withdrew to his cave of depression and fear, God visited him there. It was in this "alone" experience where he had a meeting with an angel. In *Isaiah 2:19*, it is interesting that it speaks of persons running to caves from the fearful presence of the Lord. Elijah found himself running to a cave from the fearful presence of a demonized woman, Jezebel, but ran into God's presence. *(1 Kings 19:3-11)*

Jesus could be called a "closet" man! He was always withdrawing from his disciples or the multitudes to be alone with His Father. Jesus being fully MAN knew that He needed a great amount of time to deal with the issues with His Father. It was so important for Him to do only what He saw the Father doing and what He heard from Him. It is obvious that for Jesus, this meant "closet" time. Jesus puts it this way, *"The Son can do nothing of himself, but what he seeth the Father do: for what things soever he doeth, these also doeth the Son likewise.' (John 5:19 – KJV)* There are so many references to Jesus withdrawing to pray including spending all night in prayer; forty days in fasting and in prayer (Matt 4:2; Luke 5:16; 6:12) His "closet" life obviously impressed His disciples that they turned to Him with a child-like request, *"Teach us how to pray"* (Luke 11:1)

Why The "Closet" Is A Better Place

I would like to suggest that the prayer closet is a better place to retreat to for problem- solving than the cave for the following reasons:-

o   *Meeting With God versus Meeting with Self*

The closet is a place of meeting with God; the cave is a place of meeting with self. When a man withdraws into his cave, he is looking within himself and to his own strength and self-sufficiency to solve his problems. When he withdraws to the closet, he is looking to God, enlisting God's supernatural power and might to come to bear on the situation of concern and to bring about a solution in keeping with God's plan and purposes. The Scripture does warn us about relying on ourselves as opposed to being dependent on God *(John 15:5; 2Cor 3:5; Prov. 3:5-6)*. Sometimes God will allow us to feel as if what we are facing is "killing us", not to drive us to the cave but to Him who indeed raises the dead *(2 Corinthians 1:9)*. In the closet we gain divine assurance of God's presence which eradicates all fear. We know that we have His strength, His help and His arms bearing us up. *(Isaiah 41:10)*

o   *Receiving the Wisdom of God versus Fleshly Wisdom*

In the closet we tap into the limitless wisdom of God but in the cave we tap into our own limited wisdom. The closet gives us access to God's omniscience, to His knowledge of the past the present and the future. It takes us so far beyond what we are capable of ourselves and releases word of knowledge, wisdom, discernment and revelation far beyond what we could ever attain with our own finite minds. The Bible actually calls such a person a "fool", i.e. the one who trusts in his own heart.

"He that trusteth in his own heart is a fool: but whoso walketh wisely, he shall be delivered". Prov 28:26 (KJV)

o   *Isolation versus Inclusion*

The cave is a place of seclusion; the closet is a place of inclusion. Instead of cutting ourselves off from others, we are actually meeting with the most significant persons in our lives. The King of Kings, the Lord of Lords, the God of this universe. Our Heavenly Father and our big brother. Not only are we meeting with them, but we are also availing ourselves of the help of the heavenly hosts, angels at the command of our Father, sent to minister to us the heirs of salvation. It is a place where one can chase a thousand and two ten thousand as we bring to bear the power and strength of heavenly beings to act on our behalf. *(Deut.32:30; Heb 1:14)* In response to our prayers to Him, God dispatches angels and archangels, to act on our behalf as in the case of Daniel, when angels, including an archangel, Michael, were sent with the answer to Daniel's prayer. *(Daniel 10:12)*

Isaiah 43:1-4 gives such a comforting reassurance even to us as men that Divine Presence is with us even when we pass through high waters and fire because we are precious in His eyes, and even honored, to the extent that He will give peoples in exchange for our life.

o   *Uneasy Quiet versus Sounds of Life*

The cave is quiet, the closet is noisy. In the cave we are overwhelmed and speechless as we battle with our issues. In the closet we pour out our frustrations, our concerns, our praises, our petitions to the one true GOD. It is noisy and messy in the closet like a delivery room, but still and quiet in the cave like a cemetery. Which would we prefer? One sound that we carry from the closet is the sound of faith! It seems, like David, no matter where we are when we enter, there is something about meeting with God that sparks faith. The truth is, He would not have any pleasure meeting in the closet with us if we remain devoid of it. Without this faith, it is simply impossible, not difficult, not a bit problematic, not it is a work-in-progress, but it is plainly impossible to please Him! *(Hebrews 11:1- 6)* There is an assurance and a conviction that comes in the closet that is not often present in the cave.

o   ***Divine Burden-Bearing versus Human Yoke-Carrying***

In the cave we are actually shouldering our burdens and trying to lighten them ourselves. We embrace our problem, own it and take it with us into the cave to look at it, wrestle with it and try to find a solution. It becomes the center of our attention. We focus on it and it consumes our thoughts. In the closet, we take our problems and turn them over to Jesus, laying them down at His feet and letting him bear our burdens. How liberating it is to know that we do not have to carry them ourselves, but can leave them in the hands of the Lord, for Him to solve. One of the reasons we run to the cave is that we become weary of fighting what seems like "losing battles". We feel we need to hibernate and many times it is when we feel burdened and defeated. It is there that we cry within and sometimes without.

God however provides a way out for us to break off the yokes of failure, fatigue, frustration and folly. This is not a remedy that we men often like but the One Who made us points us to this *"way of escape" (1Cor 10:13)* He says our remedy is to WAIT...upon Him*! (Isaiah 40:31)* As we wait in prayer and in His presence, our strength will be renewed, and you guys know how we hate to feel weak! Our Father promises that we will mount up again like an eagle, we will be refreshed and our movements will again be robust, confident, effective, powerful and passionate. God promises us that our "weeping", even if it is on the inside, will only endure for a while but He will ensure that our joy is restored, eventually. Even when we sin and have failed Him, His anger does not last forever and He returns favour to us - *Psalm 30:5:*

For his anger endureth but a moment; in his favour is life: weeping may endure for a night, but joy cometh in the morning. (KJV).

I would rather resist the Joy-stealer who wants me locked away in a cave than the Joy-giver, who invites me to come away into His presence for restoration and rejuvenation.

o   *Trusting in Divine Help versus Wrestling in Confusion*

The cave is a place of figuring things out; the closet is a place of trusting in God even when we do not understand. In the cave we rely on our understanding and logic. In the closet we trust God who is beyond our understanding. We understand simply that man plans his own way but He is the One Who establishes our steps *(Proverbs 16:9)* What a joy it is to know, especially as a man, that I can do ALL things once Christ is within strengthening me! *(Phill. 4:13)*

o   *Facing Imprisonment versus Obtaining Freedom*

The cave can be a place of imprisonment while the closet is a place of liberation. Men can find themselves imprisoned in a cave which can take the form of alcohol, drugs, pornography, and other addictive behaviours which ends up being destructive. The cave can also become a place of escape when men don't want to deal with realities. They can find themselves in this cave for days, weeks, months or even years. However, in the closet men can find freedom and deliverance as the Lord gives solutions and frees men to relate to their loved ones. The solution is often quicker as they receive divine help and can quickly give focus and attention to move on to deal with other affairs of life.

For all the reasons listed above men, we need to abandon the cave and relocate to the closet, the prayer closet. In doing so, we will release the full potential in us to become the powerful, effective, strong men of God that He intended us to be.

Chapter Six

Capitalizing on the Differences in How Men and Women Pray

What God has perhaps allowed in the past is no longer permitted today. God is calling men to step up to the plate and do their part in prayer. The Lord today is calling ALL of the Church to prayer....both men and women, young and old. - Dave Butts

We pondered the question of whether or not it was difficult listening to God. We engaged a few praying men with this question and tickled their minds with the question of whether they thought that it was easier for one gender to listen to / wait on God for answers to prayer than the other. The ability to listen to God is not being put forth in this book as a competition between men and women. It is merely an avenue of noting any possible differences and looking at whether or not this could help men to understand the struggles and challenges that they agree they are encountering in having a consistent prayer walk. To see how they can capitalize on these differences where they may occur.

Men Listening to God

Only a few of the men of prayer that we engaged found it easy to listen within or outside of a prayer service. Some believe that "it is a learnt discipline to listen" and that it is a matter then of personal discipline to stay in God's presence long enough to hear Him. The habit of practicing to wait which often precedes listening was not developed in them.

Another problem raised was "staying focused" while waiting on God to respond. In these days of multitudinous distractions, it would definitely be more difficult to sit quietly and focus on hearing from God. To make it a lifestyle rather than an activity that is engaged in every now and then. Our lifestyles are bombarded with the ringing of cellphones, the sounds of cable television, all types of technological gadgets and toys that our visual and auditory senses sometimes find it difficult to resist. Is there a quiet place that can be found where we can pull aside to hear the things we so desperately need to hear from the God?

Maria:

I remember when I got saved as a teen and my home was constantly buzzing with activity, including daily visitors who did not have quiet dispositions. Above that my brother worked from home as an electrical technician so my home also had the noise of radios and televisions being fixed. A common feature of homes in my community was to have a big sound system and he was the owner of one with 2 speaker boxes, each approximately 3ft x 2ft. Music would constantly be blaring through his amplifier. What does one do in such a situation? I knew that I needed to have a devotional life; that I needed a quiet place to hear God and even myself; a place of no distraction. Leaving home and going somewhere every day was out of the picture. I prayed and asked God for help. Standing on the verandah one day, I looked out and saw my brother's car in the driveway and it was locked up. A thought (a God-idea) suddenly came to me. How about making the car your "quiet place"? I did.

Daily I would disappear in the car, lying behind the front seats so no one would pass by and see me; ensuring that the windows were closed to shut out the noise. There I would have rapturous fellowship with God. I remember today some of the issues I dealt with in that car and how God answered me as I listened. One question I asked Him was why He allowed me to go through so many painful experiences in my childhood. "One day you will see" was the answer He gave to this teen crouched over in the back of a vehicle. I have lived to "see" the reason and to rejoice when He began to use those very situations that broke me to build, release and deliver others! What if I had not pressed for a solution to the distractions? What if it were not that important to me to commune with and hear from God? I do not think that I would have made the strides I did spiritually from my youth and to resist the temptations that came at me almost daily from aspiring young and older men.

Most persons pray in response to a need, a pounding desperation in their chests, a feeling that if they don't pray, something untoward might happen. The prayer then is often prompted by and fuelled with anxiety as opposed to a leading of the Holy Spirit *(Rom8:26-27)* One male intercessor admitted that, "When I'm done praying, there is the habit of quickly moving on to the next task since it's not often that I hear additional instructions from God." I wonder how many men would admit that they perhaps are not hearing from God because they are not listening – they run off to other pressing tasks or simply become distracted.

Is It Easier For Women To Listen To God?

So, is it easier or harder for men to listen to God when compared with women? Does the make-up of one gender make them prone to the discipline of listening more than the other? This subject seems to have men in prayer that we communicated with, on different sides of the fence in their response. On the one hand, some men do not think it's easier for women to listen to or wait on God for answers. However there are other men who believe that women were more prone to listening to God for the following reasons:

Nature of Women: (a) women are more intentional about listening; (b) women are more dependent, trusting, yielding, and sensitive; (c) women tend to have more patience to listen to and wait on God for answers to prayer. If the latter views are true, this would suggest that the nature or the make-up of the female gender makes it easier for them to relax and listen to God.

A Matter of Socialization: Some men believe that women are perhaps more socialized to be patient; to wait, etc. Men tend to want "To Do", that is to fix things and to get results and find solutions quickly. (I can imagine the ladies smiling as they read this line)

<u>Women Engage Their Imagination More:</u> Tanya Luhrmann wrote an article, Why Women Hear God More Than Men [www.christianitytoday.com] May 7, 2012, in addressing a similar topic. She looked at differences in socialization but from a different perspective. Luhrmann postulated that it has more to do with the imagination. In her studies as an anthropologist studying religious behaviour, she has discovered that "women pray more because women are more comfortable with their imaginations." She saw imagination as playing an important role as we talk to God and listen to Him for answers:

> *"Our culture raises men to take less joy in the imagination. Men read fewer novels. They play with children less than women do. It is important to understand this difference in socialization because sometimes men who cannot hear God feel like bad Christians. They can feel that God does not love them as much as he loves their wives, even if they know that sounds silly. My work suggests that this has more to do with the way our culture teaches them to use their minds than it does with their inherent worth. It suggests that Christians should nurture men's imaginations, and that this nurturance will help them to pray more readily, and to know God more intimately as God the Father desires."*

This takes us to the left-brain and right-brain portrayal. The concept of right brain and left brain thinking developed from the research in the late 1960s of an American, Roger W Sperry [Nobel Prize winner - 1981] who did studies in psycho biology. He discovered that the human brain has two very different ways of thinking thus the section of the brain used more will produce different orientations. Let's review studies done on the study of the brain:

> A study completed recently in December 2013 on nearly 1,000 brain scans has surprisingly confirmed what many of us thought...that there are major

differences between the male & female brain. Women's and men's brains are indeed wired in fundamentally different ways.

Men's brains tend to perform tasks predominantly on the left-side, which is the logical/rational side of the brain. Women, on the other hand, use both sides of their brains because a woman's brain has a larger Corpus Callosum, which means women can transfer data between the right and left hemispheres faster than men.

[Gender & the Brain: Differences between Women & Men, http://www.fitbrains.com/blog/women-men-brains/]

Without going into much explanation of the findings of scientific research, one could consider Luhrmann's theory aforementioned about the place of imagination in prayer. Studies have shown that men are socialized to use the left side of their brain more; hence they are thought to be "logical thinkers" more than women are. In fact, in reviewing the image of the division of the brain on the website, the right side of the brain does have the word *imagination*, along with other words used more in the context of the nature of women, e.g. intuition, feelings, daydreaming. We could safely say that if prayer is linked to "imagination" then it would not be surprising that women would do better at "listening to God" if it has a lot to do with exercising the right side of the brain.

Does that however exclude men? No. No study has shown that men are incapable of using the right side of the brain. It just takes more practice for them and it seems a willingness to cut across their cultural norms and socialization to allow the God who created their minds to use both sides in a balanced way in order to get the best results in prayer.

There is also a debate going on concerning the degree to which men and women are truly different in non-physical ways. The debate seems to be around John Gray's book, **Men Are from Mars, Women Are from Venus: The Classic Guide to Understanding the Opposite**

Sex. John Gray makes a clear distinction between the sexes. He points out that, "Not only do men and women communicate differently but they think, feel, perceive, react, respond, love, need, and appreciate differently." He also points out that, "Just as a man is fulfilled through working out the intricate details of solving a problem, a woman is fulfilled through talking about the details of her problems."

There are researchers however who seem to disagree with his viewpoint. The Guardian did an online article on a study led by Daphna Joel, a psychology professor at Tel-Aviv University. "What we show is that there are multiple ways to be male and female, there is not one way, and most of these ways are completely overlapping."

This study points out that,

> There is no sharp division between male and female brains, according to researchers who found that we are all a mixture instead.

> Scientists analysed brain scans of more than 1400 men and women and found that while some features are more common in one sex than the other, each person's brain has a unique "mosaic" of these features, as well as others seen commonly in both [http://www.theguardian.com/science/2015]

Michael Bloomfield, a psychiatrist at University College London, said that while the study found no evidence for a female or male type of brain, we need a more nuanced understanding of similarities and differences in brain structure between the sexes:

This is important, as many mental illnesses are more common in one sex over the other and we still don't understand why this is. Understanding this could well help us understand some of the biological mechanisms that give rise to these illnesses, which could then enable the development of better targeted treatments. Important questions remain, such as whether the sexes tend to have differences in brain chemistry and how this may relate to brain function.

[https://www.theguardian.com/science/2015/nov/30/brain-sex-men-from-mars-women-venus-not-so-says-new-study]

Dr. Myles Munroe gives us some insight into the dilemma that is created for men, in his book, *Understanding the Purpose and Power of Men*. He writes:

> *Yet the lines of these new roles look blurry to men as traditional and contemporary ideas eclipse— overshadowing one another—and then separate again. For example, on the one hand, men are told there is no real difference between males and females and that they are to consider women as equals. On the other hand, they are encouraged to treat women with special care and courtesy—but when they do, they are often accused of chauvinism. (p11)*

Munroe also points out, in a similar way the concern of Dr. Bloomfield. He notes the statistics of males versus females in the area of crimes. He writes:

> *The majority of crimes worldwide are committed by men. Ninety to ninety-five percent of those in prison in the United States are males. Recently, I have been amazed at the increasing numbers of boys who are involved in crime. We are seeing more and more criminal activity by males between the ages of nine and eighteen. (p13)*

One cannot help but to consider these men's concerns and to contemplate John Gray's distinctions between the sexes. There must be an explanation for certain propensities and proclivities of one gender versus another. I have my own decades of experiences with men to draw upon. These came about while growing up with three brothers, being surrounded by their frequently visiting male friends and having at one point in my life mainly males as my friends. Also relating to several godsons with whom I have a close relationship. Being surrounded by and relating to more males in Ministry than females and having lived with my husband for over fifteen years, I cannot help but to testify that in my opinion, men are different from women. The Scripture is correct. God made them "male and female". (Gen 5:2) Men need a solid definition of masculinity and women need a solid definition of femininity.

Abandonment: A man of prayer indicated that in his experience, "Prayer demands abandoning our timetables and this is perhaps more difficult for men." I think that this statement begs our male readers to pause and think about it. Are men willing to abandon their timetables for God's? I have been associated with many males who deep within their hearts, think that God moves too slowly and does not produce the results that they are looking for quickly enough. Many times there seems to be an issue of mistrust. Will God linger with the answer to prayer/solution to a complex situation before the house comes crashing down.

The term abandoning does not seem to sit well with men, especially those who have a strong need to be in control. Generally men don't like the feeling of being "out of control" in various situations. Yet, when it comes to God, He is the one Person that creation needs to worship and surrender to without restraint. Jesus puts it this way. *"If any man come to me, and hate not his father, and mother, and wife, and children, and brethren, and sisters, yea, and his own life also, he cannot be my disciple." (Lk 14:26 - KJV).*

One Minister of Religion mentioned that, "Listening to God and waiting for an answer generally takes time. So it depends on the individual - male and female - that is prepared to sacrifice the time to wait on God." The word sacrifice jumped out at me. Especially in today's world, when we expect even our answers to prayers "microwaved". The time we would spend in waiting on God for answers would be a sacrifice.

One has marveled at the way we expect instant replies to our emails and text messages. For some persons, if they are not responded to instantly, they feel insulted, offended, rejected, etc. It is amazing that persons seem to think that we all sit around doing nothing, going nowhere but waiting on each other's messages. If you were to ask an audience if this is the case they would say no. It is irrational to think that persons have nothing else to do but be checking and responding to messages. Yet I have had to explain this to individuals time and time again who are truly offended. One person even asked: "But don't they go to the bathroom? They could at least check their messages and respond while they are there." This is serious because we do take the same attitude to prayer and respond to God being offended in a similar way if He does not respond microwave-fashion.

I am not here suggesting that we have not all had one or more experiences when we wished that God could have answered our prayer more quickly since we thought our request was urgent. We have been there too. However, we have to resist this notion that answers to prayers should be for instant download. We have to trust that the timing on the answers is also working together for the good of those who love the Lord and are called to His purpose. *(Romans 8:28)*

Since both genders are busy, in multiple roles, it will cost us something to "listen to" and to "wait upon God" for answers. Sometimes it might cost us our comforts, our pleasures, our reputations, and especially men might have to resist their own impulses to run ahead of God.

Devon:

I personally do not believe that it is easier for women to "listen to God". Women are talkers and they tend to unload on God but this can be a hindrance to them waiting on him to speak.

Maria:

For whatever it is worth, it might help the men to look at the matter of "imagination" as Tanya Luhrmann pointed out. Men it is not

91

too difficult nor is it ridiculous to imagine oneself as "having coffee with God." It would not be a waste of time or playing imagination games. Instead it would add to the intimacy and bring God closer to you pulling Him into your personal space rather than seeing Him as in heaven and far removed from you. Surveys have proven that those persons who are able to imagine God being close to them and doing activities with them that are special, find more intimacy with God and are better able to hear Him when He speaks. Luhrmann writes:

> *Let me be clear. I am not suggesting that God is a product of the imagination. I am instead noting that to know God intimately, you need to use your imagination, because the imagination is the means humans must use to know the immaterial. This, by the way, is something the church fathers knew well. For Augustine, the road to God ran through the mind. It is our own peculiar era that equates the imagination with the frivolous and the unreal. That is why contemporary Christians sometimes get nervous about the word imagination.*

This is something for us to pause and reflect on and to see how this might apply to us in Christianity.

Men and Women Pray Differently

This difference in methodology was looked at in various categories – the place where men and women might choose to pray; the positions in prayer; reasons why each gender might choose to pray; how much they pray with others, express their emotions and the type of satisfaction they receive from praying.

Place Where Each Prays

Although the place where one prays does not make one holier than another, this is being examined more to establish if there are differences in where men prefer to pray than women. If there is a preference then the question arises, are men having their desires met in the literal place where they pray? Do men prefer private prayers to public prayers? Do they prefer to pray indoors or outdoors? If indoors, do they usually have a preferred part of the house? If these preferences are not being met, does this hinder prayer?

I am not sure about women, but I like to pray outdoors, surrounded by nature. Some of our praying colleagues though do not have any restrictions so they pray anywhere and anytime and hold the view that the place of prayer is often determined by convenience rather than anything else. Those who were not as fond of praying outdoors like I am, tended to pray in their living room when the family is asleep, their bedroom, study room, den or in a yard. One pastor made the observation that, "women seem to pray much in bathrooms". Men don't usually like that as a "prayer closet".

Most men have an issue doing things they do not feel equipped to do because they hate feeling incompetent. So praying in public, for some may be challenging. Private prayers may be more the context in which most men may pray. A man might be inclined to pray more at home because he is usually more comfortable praying in private or intimate settings. If a male enjoys praying aloud however, his home may not be an attractive place. The Church, a wide open field or being alone in a car, would be more conducive to that.

Postures Each Prays In

From my observation, I think women tend to kneel or prostrate themselves more. Men tend to sit or bow forward. Some may enjoy praying standing, walking or laying down. Isn't our posture in praying determined by traditional views about praying? If the custom is kneeling as is in some churches, wouldn't you find both genders inclined to kneel to pray?

The position for prayer also depends on individual's preferences and the context of (reason for) the prayer. When King David was confronted with his sin of adultery by Nathan, and the child was struck by God, David took a particular posture: *"and David fasted, and went in, and lay all night upon the earth" (2 Sam 12:16 - KJV)*. On the other hand Hanna when praying for a child, *"Hanna stood up" (1 Sam 1:9 NIV)*. One male intercessor held the view that men like to exercise command, control or dominance so positions of prayer such as lying face down would not readily be accepted as would standing or sitting upright. Women he felt will more easily try to please the person they are petitioning. In the case of David, knowing that he had sinned and it was out of divine judgement why the child was struck would have taken such a posture to appeal to God's mercy in the humblest position he could think of. A position in prayer is sometimes chosen based on what is required at the moment or what makes men comfortable.

Reasons to Pray

Here are some reasons why prayer does not seem to differ much between the genders. For some, talking to God is an everyday lifestyle venture. They will pray on site with insight. As long as God indicates that there is something to pray about, that person will pray and for whomever, even if it is a stranger. Any difference between the sexes might revolve more around their different needs. Women and men have different needs.

Women may be more inclined to pray for emotional issues and family while men would pray for material things (provision) and career issues. This I think is noteworthy because it is often said that women tend to be generally focused on more relational matters so they want to talk about their relationship with their spouse, children, etc. Men want to produce and they think of themselves as providers so their career is one of the places where they can truly feel productive and that they are fulfilling their roles as providers. It would follow naturally then that where our focus is, there our prayers would be.

Maria:

A Minister of Religion and a man of prayer commented recently that "there may be a proclivity in men to turn to prayer as last resort,

94

whereas women may be more open to pray about everything." I pondered this comment and wondered, could this be one reason why our prayer meetings seem to be filled with more women than men? Is it that women don't need an "occasion" to pray or "a feeling of desperation" to talk to God. Apart from the fact that women are talkers, could it be that their relational nature drives them to talk about anything and everything with their Lover, Jesus as they usually desire to speak to their earthly lovers in the same way? Although men are not by nature talkers, there is a scriptural mandate and place for praying about everything that has nothing to do with gender!

> *Praying always with all prayer and supplication in the Spirit, and watching thereunto with all perseverance and supplication for all saints; (Ephesians 6:18 - KJV)*

Other versions of the Bible translate this "Praying always" as praying to be done on ALL occasions and no matter what the season is in our lives. "All prayer" suggests too all manner of prayer; no restrictions! We should talk to God any time and every time we need to.

Culture/social structure may cause men to focus more on physical, natural and practical issues. This same culture has crept into the Church and therefore if men seem to be sitting around praying, they are seen as lazy or lacking ambition. If a male announced that he was being called to prayer "full time", what would be the thinking of those around? Is he just going to be sitting around praying all day? How will he then support himself and his family? Doesn't it seem like he is trying to escape from getting a job and working? Yet, in Israel in King David's time, this was a full time occupation especially for the Levites who were men. These are those that would serve in the place of intercession and worship in song as their full time occupation (1Chron. 9:13, 33, 23:5, 25:1; Neh. 10:39).

> *And their brethren, heads of the house of their fathers, a thousand and seven hundred and threescore; very able men for the work of the service of the house of God. (1Chron. 9:13)*

95

"Very able men" which means they were not serving in full-time worship and prayer because they could not work otherwise. These were not among those who were physically or otherwise challenged. I wonder if within the Church, men who may feel thus called by God would be reluctant to answer that call because of cultural pressure within Christendom. Would they feel like infidels, not because they do not believe that God could call a male as a full-time intercessor but they might not feel strong enough to go against the tide of thinking that "praying is not working". My suggestion to such men would be to answer God's call on your life to full-time ministry in whatever category He calls you and leave Him with the critics.

Praying With Others

Devon:

I think that it is easier for women to pray with others and there are other men in prayer who believe that this is more a woman's inclination. The reason is that they tend to be more sociable than men are and there are more women in the church for them to be associated with in prayer. So the tendency for women to be more relational makes it easier for them.

Maria;

It seems to me that the scarcity of men should be a driving force for men to come together to pray – at least to pray for more men to be saved. Men are indeed strengthened when they see other men with them shouldering the responsibilities in the Church. A group of men with prayer-evangelism of men on their hearts, I believe would bring great results.

Again, culture might play a big role here. In some cultures, especially those where there is a strong religious divide in corporate worship between the genders, individuals might develop a preference for praying more with their own gender, (i.e. men with men and women with women). I could recall seeing this for the first time on a missions trip to

96

Belize. At a Church we visited, everyone came together for the Bible Study but when it was time to pray, the men and women separated. It felt a little strange at first when they announced this since I was accustomed to praying with and enjoyed hearing men pray. However, as I contemplated this action, I had to conclude that there was a place for this as men would pray more comfortably with men about men-related issues and especially if there were sensitive issues.

Another reason why this gravitation to praying with the same gender would be good is the necessity to safeguard each other. Prayer bonds persons and brings even unlikely persons together. It is unadvisable for members of the opposite sex to pray together especially if it is only two of them praying. It is wise to choose a prayer partner of the same gender.

Some men prefer to pray with their wife or other family members. They set up a Family Altar. This of course is a great altar from which to petition God. I must admit however, that this practice has become a scarce one. I have come to this conclusion as I have enquired in various churches and in several courses, seminars and workshops that I have conducted within the past decade. Families are hardly praying together anymore. I strongly believe that there is still a place for the Family Altar, even more so that the family is facing increased pressures that are pulling couples and members apart. I have written about it in my first book, **ARISE...Intercessors ARISE! A Manual For the Birthing, Calling, Training and Restoration of Prayer Warriors. Outskirts Press, Inc., 2015.** I quote:

> *The Family Altar is a time set apart within the family for corporate Bible study, worship and prayer. This is an opportunity for each family member to pray; for individual family members to be prayed for regarding felt needs; for struggles, even among family members to be shared for the purpose of God's intervention and for the general needs of the family to be presented to God by this unit. It is one way of affirming and confirming that God is at the centre of a home and*

fulfilling the declaration, as Joshua did, that "as for me and my house, we will serve the Lord." (Joshua 24:15-NASB).

As a family, with the fast-paced lifestyle of both parents working and getting our son off to school on time, we have had to take our family altar to the car. It is as we spend time in traffic that our time is used in prayer and in worship. After a breakfast meal, the Scripture and a devotional reading is done. We have found that the time spent on the road is such precious quantity of time that we are unable to recoup when we are at home, especially for focused quality praying together. The car becomes that "closet" where, as a unit, we can shut out the world and speak to our Father in heaven. For prayer as a couple, my husband and I have had to find ways and means to ensure that we are able to have our personal requests aired in prayer, together. One innovative way we have adopted is on our walks together for the purpose of exercising. Though the prayers are shorter then, we are able to address and make declarations over circumstances that we are faced with.

If the Family Altar is broken down in the watchman-intercessors family, it can be repaired (1 Kings 18:30). How do you prepare this altar? By recognizing that it is broken down; confessing that it should have been erected and being serviced; invite family members to participate in this time of devotion to God, explaining the benefits of having such an Altar and being persistent in maintaining this Altar, as many things will assail the family, even to specifically, destroy this Altar. Satan hates the agreement and unity in prayer that could be experienced during these times and more so, the answers to prayer that could come to strengthen the faith of family members (p 82-83)

A pastor pointed out to me that women are "more gregarious / more open" but men are "more lone-rangers; less open / vulnerable". This is suggesting that men would normally be more private re their emotions, and would only want to pray with others when they feel comfortable. It is likely then that women would be more attuned to having a prayer partner than men. This may explain why, in our experience, it is women who speak more of having a prayer partner. I am not sure if this might have to do with homophobia since praying with a prayer partner could entail many visits / long and frequent sessions on the phone. Many males might not want to have their character or orientation in question as a result.

Expressing Emotions/ Intimacy

We must admit that men are designed differently from women and socialized differently especially in the expression of emotions. Men are more comfortable around other men and learn better around other men. It is often said that women are more emotional than men and this is one reason why females get more out of spending longer times in the closet of prayer. They are seen to be usually crying, pouring out a lot of their feelings, etc. thus making prayer somewhat easier for them. Women definitely are more inclined to do this; they are far more expressive emotionally than are men. Men mostly express emotions associated with calm, control or dominance. Although we are saying that men are less expressive emotionally both in words and body language, let's keep it in the context of the subject matter of praying. Men are certainly very emotional in their expressions when it comes to sports and competitive activities.

We must not forget though that there are still exceptions. For example, one pastor who we spoke with expresses emotions more when he prays alone or with his wife. He hardly gets emotional otherwise. My own experience with Devon is that he speaks a lot more to me than with other men and therefore expresses more of his feelings with me. He prays more with me too than with other men.

One Jamaican pastor shared with us that "Jamaican men are restrained generally, re expressing certain emotions. They will however do so if they feel safe and helped to do so." I found this comment interesting because of my personal experience. When Devon and I were courting, based on his background, he hardly spoke about his emotions. However, as time went by, he began to see the necessity for this especially when building an intimate relationship. Within our marriage, the more he expressed and the more I responded, the deeper our marriage grew. I wonder if this is not also true of our relationship with the Lord. The more men can abandon themselves in His presence, expressing their true emotions, the more their relationship with God will grow. As was pointed out earlier, the issue of abandonment is more of a challenge for men. But I would want our readers to examine their prayer life to see how much they really express their deep emotions in prayer. To ask themselves if prayer would be more meaningful and their relationship with Jesus become even more intimate if they would truly abandon themselves before Him.

My favourite Old Testament character is a male. David has always been an inspiration to me since my youth. I have understood a lot about praying and relating intimately with God through David and especially studying the Psalms. Who would not want to learn why God said of him that he was a man after His own heart. (Acts 13:22) But what were some of the reasons why God viewed him in this way. Ron Edmondson who serves as the senior pastor of Immanuel Baptist Church in Lexington, Kentucky, suggested 10 Reasons why David was seen in this light by God.

- Humble – ... Psalm 62:9
- Reverent -... Psalm 18:3
- Respectful – Be merciful to me, O Lord, for I am in distress; my eyes grow weak with sorrow, my soul and my body with grief. Psalm 31:9
- Trusting – ... Psalm 27:1
- Loving – I love you, O Lord, my strength. Psalm 18:1
- Devoted – You have filled my heart with greater joy than when their grain and new wine abound. Psalm 4:7

- o Recognition – I will praise you, O Lord, with all my heart; I will tell of all your wonders. Psalm 9:1
- o Faithful – ... Psalm 23:6
- o Obedient – ....Psalm 119:34
- o Repentant – .... Psalm 25:11

"David's example is a great road map for how we are to live our life."

[http://www.biblestudytools.com/blogs/ron-edmondson/10-reasons]

I have chosen to highlight some of the Scriptures he quoted because I believe that they are expressive of David's emotions. I see him expressing love, joy, and praise with all his heart. We also know of many where he expressed grief and fear. (Psalm 34:4-5; 51; 54:1) How could such a warrior express such tender feelings towards his Lord; move away from the fields of battle to be intimate with his Creator; get past his weakness and fallen nature to reconnect with a forgiving God and put aside his macho character to abandon himself to the grace and mercy of his Heavenly Father. I believe that this is a great bible character for all men of God to study. In his relationship with God, he is a good expression of the lion and the lamb. So I wondered why men in general would have a problem expressing emotions and how this book could help them to understand themselves. I wanted to see what men had to say about other men. Take this journey with me.

Reasons Men Find it Difficult to Express Their Emotions

John M. Grohol, Psy.D. indicated in an article that, "Saying how you feel is something you can learn how to do, just as readily as you can learn how to fix a faucet...". He gives several reasons why men (and people in general) might have problems expressing emotions. Some of the areas on his list were:

- • Conflict Phobia - You are afraid of angry feelings or conflicts with people
- • Passive-Aggressive Behavior - ...a common strategy to elicit feelings of guilt (on their part).

- Mind Reading - You believe that others should know how you feel and what you need (although you have not disclosed what you need).
- Need to Solve Problems - When you have a conflict with an individual (i.e., your needs are not being met), avoiding the associated issues is not a functional solution. Disclosing your feelings and being willing to listen without judgment to the other is constructive. [http://psychcentral.com/lib/10-reasons-you-cant-say-how-you-feel/]

I have chosen to highlight these because of my experience as a professional counsellor, where these barriers are very commonly seen in men. Many men, whether in a group counselling context or in private counselling, have disclosed to me that they really don't like conflict. Sometimes, it may seem like a paradox but, they may even "create" a scene to throw off an impending or perceived upcoming conflict. They just don't want to be involved in an emotional web and face conflicts head-on so instead they take evasive action that avoids the conflict as opposed to processing and constructively confronting it. This makes me wonder if this "conflict phobia" that Dr. Grohol alludes to may explain too why men may not run to prayer at times, i.e. out of a fear that their request might not meet divine approval or activate divine release of a needed or desired answer. They fear that their request may come into conflict with what God desires for their lives. Avoidance then becomes the escape route.

Mind-reading expectations is another barrier I have seen. This is the assumption that the other party should know what you want and how you are feeling without you having to inform them or repeat yourself, especially if there was a similar occurrence some time before. Men, more than women have wondered and expressed to me a baffling question. Why do I have to repeat my request to God when he already knows that I am in need? A humorous picture from the bible comes to mind when I hear this question being asked. A man, obviously blind, stands before Jesus, the Healer. Jesus asks him, "What can I do for you?" (Mark 10:51) When I share this account, I usually indicate that it is not ridiculous to ask someone who seems to be in some obvious need, what

102

to pray for or how you could help them. Did it ever occur to you that the blind man could have told Jesus that he wanted a wife! Or that his need for companionship could have been greater than his need to see? The counselling room is where you get the surprises. You certainly learn to listen and not jump to conclusions; not make hasty judgements from what you see or hear on the surface. It is obvious that God has laid out His divine principle. We must humbly ask for what we need.

- *Matthew 7:7 - Ask, and it shall be given you; seek, and ye shall find; knock, and it shall be opened unto you*
- *Matthew 21:22 - And all things, whatsoever ye shall ask in prayer, believing, ye shall receive*
- *John 16:24 - Hitherto have ye asked nothing in my name: ask, and ye shall receive, that your joy may be full.*

The Bible even points out that there are ways to ask, e.g. that we should not be wavering in any way. This will not bring any success in prayer. (James 1:6-8) We have already dealt with the issue of the need to solve their own problems and many times instantly, which creates a lot of bundling in the minds and lives of men.

Type of Satisfaction Received From Praying

One of the things that will draw us back to an experience is the level of satisfaction that we get from it. We are a pleasure-oriented people and it is divine discipline or a choice to discipline ourselves for a greater cause that will make us persist in an event that is in the process, void of personal satisfaction. Men do receive some satisfaction from prayer or they would not do it. They may perceive this satisfaction in ways different from women. Men may speak to peace of mind, etc. Prayer is cathartic in releasing pent up stress. Men are more inclined to be satisfied by the result of prayer – even as a tension-reliever. A man can find "peace, guidance and status as leader from praying", as one pastor shared.

Another pastor who took one of our courses on Intercession had an interesting perspective that he found satisfying in prayer. He found that: "Prayer changes me to deal with situations". Wow! There are very few persons that I have heard in my over three decades of being involved with leading prayer groups and ministries, who rejoice and find satisfaction in the fact that prayer changes them! The focus is usually on how prayers can change others to become what we desire them to be and on changing circumstances that somehow challenge our comfort-zones. I wonder what Christendom would be like now if we all, male and female, young and old, pursue prayer as God's vehicle to bring personal change and Christlikeness into our souls.

There is one aspect that cannot be left out when we speak of satisfaction. What about our Lord? Does He want us to have satisfaction in the activity of prayer or does He want us to "sweat it out", be dry, unfulfilled and feeling as if this is always a "sacrifice" we have to make? The Bible tells us that *"in thy presence is fullness of joy; at thy right hand there are pleasures for evermore." (Ps 16:11 – KJV)*. The more an individual is committed to praying and most especially in the spirit and in submission to the leading of the Holy Spirit, the more the satisfaction one derives from praying.

What If I Am Not Feeling Satisfied in My Prayer Life

So men, if you are experiencing dissatisfaction in your prayer closet, you may need the Holy Spirit outpoured in your life and He getting more of you as you will be getting more of Him. Here are some steps that you could take to enrich your prayer experience and to stand strong as a man of prayer:

a) **Returning to Your First Love**: This first directive could sound like a mushy "emotional" response that you are being advised to follow except that it was Jesus' command when addressing the Church at Ephesus (Rev. 2:4). He had a complaint against them – they had left their First Love! Their passion for God had waned and their initial zeal for His presence and the Word had dwindled significantly. What were they supposed to do since they were working hard for the Lord and doing the right things but not experiencing the "joy" of their salvation as they used to?

One of the things that I have found in counselling couples that often stimulates their passion and rekindle their love is to ask, "How did you meet and what attracted you to him/her in the beginning?" There is usually a smile that comes to the face; a twinkle in the eye; a shifting in the seat as he/she reminisces. They remember the heart-throbbing, heart-skip-a-beat, palm-sweating moments of excitement. Men might not describe their initial salvation experience in exactly those terms but it is important to "keep the fire going in our hearts" like it was burning when we just met the Lord. Repentance and renewal therefore are the first steps. One has to take a right-about turn and go back in the direction of loving God with all our heart, soul, mind and strength. (Luke 10:27)

And he answered, *"YOU SHALL LOVE THE LORD YOUR GOD WITH ALL YOUR HEART, AND WITH ALL YOUR SOUL, AND WITH ALL YOUR STRENGTH, AND WITH ALL YOUR MIND; AND YOUR NEIGHBOR AS YOURSELF."* [New American Standard Bible]

The question is what has distracted us and drawn our attention away from our enamouring focus that we once had on our God? We have to "go back" to the place where we first believed.

The more we get to know someone, the more we can get to truly love them. The greater the understanding of who they are, where they are coming from and what causes them to do what they do, the more we want to draw closer. Get to know God for yourself. Dig into the Scriptures to learn more of Him and watch that love and appreciation for Him grow again.

b) **Make God the Priority Again**: One of the hardest things to be honest about is admitting to oneself that God is not truly priority in our lives. Preference and greatest importance goes to someone or something else – not Him. How that must break His heart to see Himself slipping down the ladder of priorities in our lives. Ever played a game of Snake and Ladder and just as you are at the top, heading home, you are swallowed by that big ugly snake that takes you way to the bottom! If men can begin by admitting this error of allowing that demonic serpent to swallow up their time, attention and priority that God should be getting in their lives; if they can humble themselves, choosing to purposefully take back God to the top while pulling down the idols, because that's what they really are. Anything that is placed before or ahead of God is an idol. If they can do these things while avoiding the serpent that is waiting to pull them back into all types of distractions, they will begin to experience some victory over dryness and dissatisfaction in their prayer walk.

c) **Be Relentless in Removing the Things That Hurt God**: We know when we hurt the one we love, especially when we know them well enough to know their likes and dislikes. So it is with God. We know from the Scriptures when we are hurting him and as a result, hurting ourselves and others. Sin dulls our spiritual sensing. It removes our excited anticipation to get in the presence of God. It brings a shadow and cloud of shame that seem to follow us everywhere. It takes us away from God! We have to be persistent and deliberate in the fight against sin until we have victory over every bit of it.

I always find it interesting, when I read of David's repentance in Psalm 51. Here he has hurt a family by taking the wife for himself and ordering the murder of her husband. At the end, he regains the right perspective – Who it was that he ultimately had hurt:

> *Against You, You only, I have sinned And done what is evil in Your sight, So that You are justified when You speak And blameless when You judge.*

> *(Psalm 51:4 – NASB)*

d) **Recognize the Heart Matters That Often Affect our Passion**: Depression, discouragement, disappointment, and death of a significant person to us, may bring about a dampening or deadening of once vibrant emotions and decrease in our spiritual "energy". One way that I have often explained this is to use the analogy of having a bad flu. During such an illness, one is usually affected at all levels – the energy to do spiritual and physical things has diminished and one does not have the appetite for pleasurable things as was the case before the illness. In dealing with this issue in my book, **ARISE...Intercessors Arise!** I wrote:

> *Romans 8:26 – 28 tells us that "the Spirit also helpeth our infirmities: for we know not what we should pray for as we ought : but the Spirit itself maketh intercession for us.."(KJV) Jesus made it very clear that the Holy Spirit is given to us as a Paraclete which means an advocate or helper. Since the arm of flesh cannot fulfil the purposes of God, this Paraclete is sent to teach us all things. (John 14:26) and to help us where we are weak. The word 'infirmities" comes from the Greek word, astheneia which means, "want of strength", "weakness", indicating inability to produce results. A raw translation of the phrase in Greek is "takes share in the weakness of us". What a precious gift that is given to the Christian and to those who are called to be watchmen-intercessors.*

Some possible infirmities/weaknesses could be conscious iniquity of our hearts when we come to pray; ignorance concerning the will of God; physical weakness – infirmity in our bodies, which impact on the "strength" that we need to persevere in prayer and the struggle against Satan who seeks to oppress or depress or to create doubt, disillusionment and discouragement. (p 43)

The Rom. 8:26-28 passage is a great encouragement to all Christians that whatever the weakness or state of weakness that we are in, God has provided a Helper for us. That Helper is the Holy Spirit who you can turn to anywhere and at any time that you are experiencing weakness. He understands. He can identify. He is that great Advocate Who can make up for our weaknesses by strengthening us to pray and to do the will of God.

e) **Receive a Passion For Soul-Winning and Missions**: There seems to be a correlation between our zeal for soul-winning and the excitement that we experience in the closet. If a mission to the lost is not one of the burning petitions that we are lifting up to God then our prayer life becomes self-indulgent which brings a diminishing satisfaction. One thing that men like is to produce. If their lives are not producing "children for God" then there can be an emptiness or even demotivation in doing the other religious activities. There is nothing like having a burning passion that is birthed as a result of answering God's call on a daily basis. Seeing those who we have been praying for and witnessing to, sometimes for years, finally make that bold step to begin to serve the Lord in fullness. Doesn't that excite more praying... wanting to see more souls come to the Lord even through our petitioning Him? Prayer then becomes the important vehicle to ensure that we hear God's instructions; that we receive His anointing; that we are empowered every day as He orders our steps. As one article puts it:

Not only do you have the ear of the greatest Person in the universe, but has it ever occurred to you, as you kneel in your place of prayer, that you have been given the privilege of being used of God to help change the lives of individuals and nations. God has literally made available to you His vast reservoir of power, wisdom, love and grace, if only you are willing to believe him, to trust and obey Him." [www.cru.org/train-and-grow/transferable-concepts/pray-with-confidence.]

f) **Get Rid of Worry – Another Passion-Eater**: Years ago, I heard a famous preacher-author say, "There is nothing that God made in our bodies to withstand worry" That was a Selah moment for me. Seriously. It is true. God does not even encourage a little worry. The Scripture just tells us bluntly, "BE ANXIOUS FOR NOTHING"! (Phill 4:6) Isn't it natural to worry over something or someone at some point? There is nowhere in Scriptures that gives us such "luxury". There is always an antidote that the Scripture recommends which is found in that passage:

Be anxious for nothing, but in everything by prayer and supplication with thanksgiving let your requests be made known to God. [NASB]

Prayer…supplication…and definitely not leaving out the thanksgiving, we are to make our requests be known to Him. Does this sound too simple an answer for the types of burdens that we carry? Well, this is God's answer. Many over the centuries, including us, have proven that the place of prayer is the best place to dump all our worries!

We hope that at this point, you are already feeling encourage to revisit that passion that you once had for God. We hope that you are saying with the songwriter: "Take me back dear Lord where I first received You; Take me back dear Lord where I first believed." The Holy Spirit is waiting on that petition and He is willing to do just that for you.

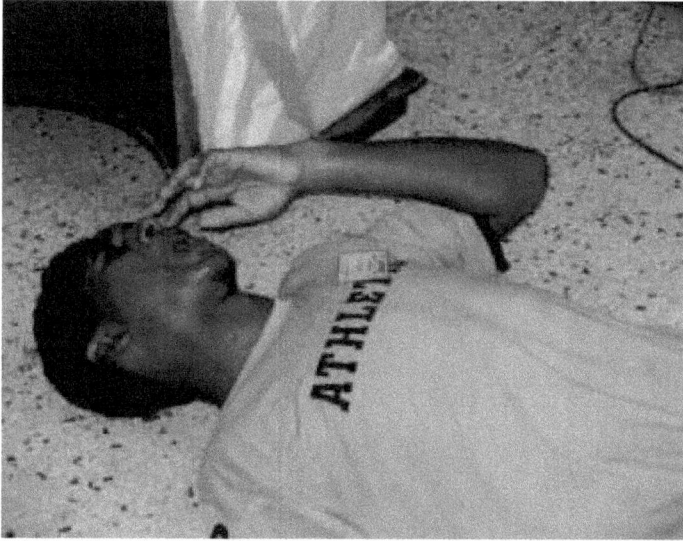

D. Thomas, a youth crying out to God for his peers at annual Intercessors Camp in Jamaica

Chapter 7

The Man That God Desires

"Solid character will reflect itself in consistent behavior, while poor character will seek to hide behind deceptive words and actions." — *Myles Munroe*

DAVID AND SAUL

Weaknesses Versus Self-Will

The account of these two men, Saul and David, are worthy of in-depth studying. For our purposes, we are attempting to glean from what God had to say about both, whether directly or through His prophets, His esteem of their lives. They had some similarities:

- Both were Jews and grew up knowing God's Law – those given to Moses
- Both were called by God to serve as Israel's leader(1 Sam 9:16, 17; 16:1, 12)
- Both were anointed under God's instructions, by a prophet (1 Sam 10:1; 16:13)
- Both came from humble backgrounds – there was no notoriety prior to their elevation to the throne of Israel (1 Sam 9:21; 15:17; 2 Sam 12:7, 8)
- Both were men of war (1 Sam 18:7)
- Both fell into some kind of sin and failed God
- Both had major consequences applied to their lives as a result of their sin (1 Sam 15:22, 23; 2 Sam 12:10-14)

With all of these similarities, the end of each life had different commentaries. One life was celebrated by God, highlighted positively by Jesus, used as a positive source for teaching others how to respond to God while the other became a byword. How could this be? Let us look more closely at their lives.

The Type of Man That God Rejects - KING SAUL

King Saul began as a humble man, feeling unworthy and somewhat incapable of leading God's people. (1 Sam 9:21; 10:21-22) He learnt in the beginning of his kingly career to depend on God's leading, through His prophet Samuel. (1 Sam 13:8) There was a dependency on God and initially he could recognize someone with God's anointing, hence he called David to live in the palace and to play skillful music for him when he was being tormented and to go out to battle against Goliath in the Name of the Lord (1 Sam 16:18 -19; 17:37).

A great beginning but the type of heart he had came out eventually. His character which was his "true colours" came out progressively when he refused to take control of his weaknesses – the type that led him to sin and to be unrepentant before God. He could not deal with competition, another person being celebrated more than him; he did not deal with his fears. Those fears later became his downfall.

The man that God does not desire takes some dangerous turns in life without waiting on God and seeking His face in prayer. And when his error(s) are pointed out, he allows pride and arrogance to take over as opposed to allowing the Spirit of the Lord to work repentance in him! What a tragedy when we allow "the flesh", our self-will and our foolish disposition that we can outdo God, get in the way of His free and willing divine help for those who are broken and contrite in spirit.

One criterion that we know for sure that God has for accepting or rejecting a man has to do with his heart. *1Sam 16:7:*

> *"But the LORD said unto Samuel, Look not on*
> *his countenance, or on the height of his stature; because*
> *I have refused him: for the LORD seeth not as man*

112

seeth; for man looketh on the outward appearance, but the LORD looketh on the heart." (KJV)

What were some of these "turns" in King Saul's life that jeopardized his walk with God and seemed to have removed him from being "God's man"?

Unbridled Sin – Jealousy

His jealousy for David being allowed to get out of control – running unbridled! Mankind, whatever the gender and whether Christian or not, struggles with jealousy at one time or another. As a matter of fact, David himself seemed to have had stints of jealousy especially when he saw the wicked prospering (Psalm 37:1; 73:3) The feeling of jealousy and his competitive nature as a warrior were not the real problems. It was how he handled it. I believe if he had humbled himself and confessed that he saw David as a threat and asked God to help him to deal with the jealousy that was now flooding his heart; he would have received divine help, strength and the ability to be an overcomer. Saul chose to do the opposite and this was what led to his downfall and the receiving of divine disapproval and rejection. Firstly, when he heard the

The man that God does not desire takes some dangerous turns in life without **waiting** on God and **seeking His face in prayer**. And when his error(s) are pointed out, he allows **pride** and **arrogance** to take over as opposed to allowing the Spirit of the Lord to work repentance in him!

women celebrating David's prowess over his, he allowed himself to boil over with anger and allowed his heart to become so bitter towards him to the point of planning and attempting his murder. (1 Sam 18:8-11; 19:1)

I could hear someone asking: But didn't David also plan and execute a murder, Uriah's? Yes, as mentioned before, both men fell into some kind of grave sin and failed God but the difference was that when each was confronted with his sin, one sincerely repented while the other pretended to change initially, but became more and more presumptuous as he went along to the point of slaying eighty-five of God's priests who he perceived were protecting David. Afterwards, he slew all others, even the animals (1 Sam 22:16-19). The difference would lie in the one who truly experienced godly sorrow and bore fruit of repentance and the one who didn't. Saul had "repented" more than once for wanting to do David, a good and godly man evil yet he continued to pursue him to kill him! (1 Sam 24:16-22; 26:21-25)

Disrespect for Divine Boundaries

Saul makes sacrifice overstepping his bounds and role as a king.(1 Sam 13:8 – 14) Again being human, he became afraid when (a) the person who embodied for him, divine help, the prophet Samuel did not show up within seven days; (b) the people of his kingdom began to "scatter from him" (interestingly a similar scenario to David fleeing from Israel when his son Absalom planned a coup against him). (c) His enemies, the Philistines had assembled against him. Again, fear is common to man but it is what we do with our fears. Saul chose to overstep God's limits and offer the sacrifice that only the priest was permitted to offer. That incurred God's wrath and God acted against him. I believe the prophet Samuel's utterance to Saul following this act were words that no child of God would want to hear:

> [13] *And Samuel said to Saul, Thou hast done foolishly: thou hast not kept the commandment of the Lord thy God, which he commanded thee: for now would the Lord have established thy kingdom upon Israel forever.*

[14] But now thy kingdom shall not continue: the Lord hath sought him a man after his own heart, and the Lord hath commanded him to be captain over his people, because thou hast not kept that which the Lord commanded thee.   [1 Samuel 13:13-14 (KJV)]

What is heart-breaking and would cut to the core of a man's heart is that God was offering him power forever – even through his lineage! *"...for now would the Lord have established thy kingdom upon Israel forever."* There is no record of Saul repenting and asking God for mercy. The following verse (15) showed Saul continuing with business as usual and numbering his men!

The second account of Saul overstepping divine boundaries was just as devastating. (1 Sam 15) He now got to the point when it was not fear that propelled him to disobey God but self-will. He totally ignored the instructions of Samuel the prophet which he knew were from God. (15:3, 9) He was now a law unto his own self. It seemed power had corrupted him because his heart was not right before God. He was a backslider! (15:11) He began to blame the people for his own disobedience (15:15); he did evil in God's sight (15:19); he lied to the man of God, Samuel (15:20) **THERE IS STILL NO TRUE REPENTANCE TAKING PLACE.** Saul was more concerned about how he would look in the eyes of the people – man's opinion – than the fact that he was experiencing divine anger and rejection (15:30) It was the prophet, Samuel, who corrected Saul's disobedience by executing king Agag.

Backslidden to the Point of Entertaining the Occult

Saul backslides to the point of entertaining the occult in his life – going to a witch who was hiding from him because he had driven all the mediums and wizards from the land. (1 Sam 28:3 – 25) Another law of God broken. Another act he did out of self-will and a non-repentant heart. So he asks this medium to communicate with the now dead Samuel. God allows an apparition that rebuked him and reminded him, again of words that should pierce like a knife and should be instructive to men who truly desire God:

a) The Lord had turned from him and become his enemy(28:16)

b) The Lord had torn away from Him what He had originally given to Him AND had already given it to another (28:17)

c) The Lord was about to give Israel and him into the hands of his initially defeated enemies, the Philistines. His death and the death of his sons in that war would be sure. (28:19)

Even at this point, when his life was about to end, it was fear that entered him and not repentance. I know you might be wondering, what would have happened at this stage, if he truly repented. Would he have received divine mercy? I think so. If Jezebel's wicked husband, King Ahab, received mercy from God when he humbled himself (he too was guilty of shedding innocent Naboth's blood in order to acquire his vineyard) yet when Ahab humbled himself before the Lord and truly repented, God changed His mind about some of the judgement He had spoken against him! (1 Kings 21:27 – 29)

The Type Of Man That God Desires – KING DAVID

You would have already picked up from the negative attitudes and actions in Saul's life that led to God rejecting him, what are some of the things that God looks for in the man that He desires and accepts. Again, if we could sum it up – it is an issue of the heart. (1 Sam 16:7)

What then were some of the things in David's Heart that led God to choose Him over Saul; to establish his kingdom forever; to choose his lineage to bring forth the Messiah and to call him "a man after his own heart" although he had messed up in various ways, the primary ones being adultery leading to murder. *Acts 13:22 (KJV):*

> *And when he had removed him, he raised up unto them David to be their king; to whom also he gave their testimony, and said, I have found David the son of Jesse, a man after mine own heart, which shall fulfill all my will.*

The truth is that when one studies David's life, one could find many weaknesses, especially in his family life. The primary weakness

116

seemed to be his inability to manage his own household and to appropriately deal with his children when they had sinned against God or each other. So Amnon, having raped his half-sister and causing her to be banished to desolation for life, was never rebuked or aptly punished but his brother, Absalom, who took revenge on Amnon for his action, was banished for years from the king's presence. Nevertheless, David still stands out as a favourite character for believers, in the Old Testament and a lauded favourite of God in his lifetime. What kind of disposition did he have that allowed God to favour him?

A Heart After God – Clearing Himself of Guilt

This heart after God was more than just about how he worshipped God. It had also to do with his humility with men. Because of David's heart, he was spared several times from blood-guiltiness. Yes, David had killed Uriah innocently and was guilty of shedding innocent blood. This act was never overlooked by God but because of David's repentant heart, after the fact, God forgave him. Consequences followed the sin, but God's mercy showed up for him because of his heart.

Many occasions presented itself, before he ascended the throne and while he was king, for him to kill and heap blood-guilt on his head but he refused to. Some of these occasions included, (a) His relenting from killing Nabal who had mishandled his men, after Nabal's wife, Abigail, appealed to David not to shed innocent blood. (1 Sam 25:26, 33); b) One two occasions he had King Saul at his mercy and could have killed this man who was pursuing him to kill him. Wouldn't that have been self-defence. Yet David refused to "touch the Lord's anointed" – the man who God had set up as king over His people. David restrained himself and his men from killing Saul twice. (1 Sam 24:4 -7) and (1Sam 26:9-12)

Upholding and Esteeming God's Word – Brokenness When Sinned

If there was a man who truly loved God's law, it was David. (*Ps 119:27, 97 - KJV*):

> [27] *Make me to understand the way of thy precepts: so shall I talk of thy wondrous works.*

> [97] *O how love I thy law! it is my meditation all the day*

However, in spite of this love for God's Law, David allowed lust to consume his heart, and he fell into sin. Many of God's men can identify with David. What made David unique and what makes every man of God and of prayer, special, is how the struggle with sin and their "fall" are handled.

David's Brokenness

When David was confronted with his sin by the prophet Nathan, instead of being defensive and continuing the deception, he quickly admitted to wrongdoing, confessed before God and humbled himself before the one who was confronting him with truth.

> *And David said unto Nathan, I have sinned against the Lord. And Nathan said unto David, The Lord also hath put away thy sin; thou shalt not die. (2 Sam 12:13 – KJV)*

The level of brokenness that he felt when he realized how he had hurt the Lord is enlightening to men of God. Psalm 51 sums up this process very well. (a) He begins with an appeal to God for mercy – the full-blown reality of what He had done moved him to cry out for what He knew he did not deserve but also knowing that God's character was Mercy personified. (vs 1-3) (b) He recognizes that more than what he has done to men, he has offended a holy God whose judgement would have been righteous. (v 4) (c) He faces now the truth that one must grapple with – who am I really? What propels me to do the things that I do? (James 1:13f) What does God require of me? David seemed almost shocked at himself and with what he did (his sin). So he cries out for **truth** and **wisdom** to be rooted deep within his heart. (vs 6-10) (d) The last thing that David wanted to lose and the only thing He knew he could not do without was God's presence through His Holy Spirit. "Cast me not away" he cried out.

It is obvious that David had encountered the Holy Spirit and God's holy presence enough to value and cherish them. Any man of God, who has experienced the fullness of God's presence and is now feeling the blow of possibly losing God's Holy Spirit as a result of "grieving" Him, would cry out for Him to stay and would be willing to do whatever it takes to make it happen. If there was anyone who watched first-hand what could happen to a man who loses the Holy Spirit, it is David. He watched the disintegration of King Saul as a result. (1 Sam 16:14; 19:9) We could speculate that Saul's end might have been plaguing David's thoughts – how the kingdom was ripped from Saul; how God stopped responding to his prayer and how God stopped protecting him from his enemies. A man of God like David, being in his right mind, would not want to embrace such a future! David knew brokenness. God responded to his broken spirit and contrite heart which God never despises. (Ps 51:17) We could conclude then that true brokenness moves the heart of God even when we fail Him.

Unshakeable Trust in God – Even When Faced With His Enemies

David had a trust in God that neither time nor circumstances could shake. This was a trust that he learnt from fighting wild animals and experiencing victory over them. (1 Sam 17:34 - 36) A trust that made him know as he faced Goliath that he was, as someone once said, "too big to miss"! (1 Sam 17:45 – 50) It's a trust that kept him as he fled from Saul, in caves, valleys, in the camp of the Philistines, etc. (1 Sam 18 – 26)

We will hasten to say that David's unshakeable trust in His God had much to do with the fact that he was a **Man of Prayer**. Whenever he was confronted with his enemies, he consulted God. What shall I do? When he lost everything at Ziklag and fear could have overtaken him after his own men in their grief, plotted to stone him, he turned to God in prayer and looked to God for strength. (1 Sam 30:6-8) The ultimate test might have been when he was driven from the kingdom by his own son Absalom, later to be stoned by a non-entity. Again he threw himself at God's mercy and restrained his men from killing his assailant, Shimei. (2 Sam 16:5-11) Many of the psalms are replete with David's absolute trust in the character of God. (Psalm 20:7; 25; 31; 37:3-5)

MORDECAI AND HAMAN

Power and Pride versus Prostration

Again, one can see a striking contrast between two men, one initially with only spiritual authority and the other with natural power being an official of the king. One man depended on the power that he had through position but the other the power he had with God! One man who could not be satisfied with all of his accolades until he could be treated like a god; the other with no accolades but knew that he and his God made a majority and together they could bring down any kingdom.

Power and Arrogance Corrupts

The man that God would reject is Haman. Haman the Agagite, or "Haman the evil one" was antagonistic towards the Jews. He was a vizier in the Persian empire under King Ahasuerus, which was a high officer in a Muslim government. (www.thefreedictionary.com) Haman, chief minister of the king (Es.3:1-2) was a descendant of Agag, the king of the Amalekites. He relentlessly attempted to exterminate the Jews in the kingdom of Ahasuerus and he became one of the earliest persecutors of the Jews. He had a wicked heart:

(a) Filled with annoyance because Mordecai did not bow before him, Haman resolved to exterminate the Jews throughout the whole kingdom, no matter the cost. (b) Haman used bribery - He offered the king ten thousand talents of silver to carry out his plan against the Jews. (3:9) Permission was granted and letters with the king's signature sent to the different parts of the Persian kingdom to massacre the Jews. (3:12 – 14)

His tormented spirit would not be at peace until he could get Mordecai to bow or to die! (c) Overcome with arrogance and a false sense of victory, he prepared a gallows whereon to hang Mordecai (5: 14).

The Scripture tells us that pride comes before destruction and an arrogant spirit before a fall (Prov 16:18) The events following his victory with the king and his diabolical plan against Mordecai is about to backfire. The king calls him and enquires what should be done to someone whom the king delights to honour. Haman so full of self-importance and pride assumed that the king was referring to him. He therefore gave it his best shot ensuring that he highlighted the most honourable demonstration of royal approval that anyone below the king could receive. To his shock and amazement, his arch enemy, Mordecai, was the person who the king delighted to honour. (6:6 – 12) To add insult to injury, it was Haman who was delegated the responsibility to robe Mordecai and march him through the streets displaying the king's honour upon him. His legs were perhaps the heaviest ever and his speech almost challenged as he had to lead that procession declaring that Mordecai was being honoured by the king. He quickly clings to the demonic counsel of his wife, Zeresh. She prompted and encouraged Haman to build a gallows for Mordecai which would lead to the defeat of this enemy, once and for all.

Esther then invites Haman and the king to a banquet. He might have assumed in his self-importance and arrogance that he was being honoured above all others, to be the sole one selected to accompany the king. It was at this banquet that Esther exposed to the king, Haman's plot to destroy the Jews. The king was filled with anger upon hearing this, but even more so that Haman fell upon the queen's couch where she was seated. The king ordered his officers to hang Haman on the gallows which he had prepared for Mordecai. (7:7 - 10)

Prostration Which Leads to Exaltation

The Scripture tells us that God resists the proud and gives grace to those who humble themselves before Him (Jas 4:6). It therefore means that there are those who God desires and responds to their plea for

121

help and to some, He doesn't. Mordecai was never looking for exaltation. His main concern was rescuing his people. So there are some things that should be noted about this man of God who God accepts and uses an earthly king to honour. Oftentimes when the account of Esther is repeated, the self-sacrifice is brought out in favour of Esther, sometimes overlooking the first one who truly began to lay down his life. It is said of Mordecai that he, in response to the news of the edict that was sent out against his people, took an action that was certainly not flattering to his image and reputation.

> *When Mordecai learned what had been done, he ripped his clothes to shreds and put on sackcloth and ashes. Then he went out in the streets of the city crying out in loud and bitter cries. He came only as far as the King's Gate, for no one dressed in sackcloth was allowed to enter the King's Gate. As the king's order was posted in every province, there was loud lament among the Jews—fasting, weeping, wailing. And most of them stretched out on sackcloth and ashes.*
>
> *Esther's maids and eunuchs came and told her. The queen was stunned. She sent fresh clothes to Mordecai so he could take off his sackcloth but he wouldn't accept them...*   *(Esther 4:1-4 - MSG)*

This was a respectable man in the community, ripping his clothes, putting on certainly not an attractive garment (sackcloth), dousing himself with ashes and crying bitterly. Not an image with which men would readily want to identify. The fact that Queen Esther was sending fresh clothes for him to adorn himself tells us that it was unsightly. The donning of sackcloth in that era depicted a condition of one's heart and the burden of a soul before God. The situation had to be a grievous one for men of God to dress accordingly. He first modeled what he was requiring of Esther. He led by example.

Knows How to Prioritize God's Kingdom

This surrogate father's challenge to his relative Esther was a challenge to put God's business, His kingdom and His people first! To step away from her comfort-zone and to deal with the business of the King of all kings. Mordecai's challenge in Esther 4:12-14 would be a parallel to Jesus' exhortation to believers to seek first *His* kingdom. (Matt 6:33) This is what would attract God to a man – the fact that He is concerned about the things that concerns the King. Mordecai's role as a praying man was evident by the extent to which he went to cry out to God and to petition man (Esther) to change.

Which king would not, in the natural, be drawn to and consider giving favour to a subject who places the business of his kingdom as priority. Earthly kings do it and even more so our King of kings. He in fact automatically causes all other things that we need to be added to our lives. (Matt 6:33)

It was Mordecai's prayer life (in the closet) that made him be able to stand boldly to confront the situation that was threatening his people. I have dealt with this topic in my book, **ARISE...Intercessors Arise** (p10). I quote:

> *The Edict went out – "Kill all the Jews." (Esther 4:7, 8). The intercessor in Mordecai rose up in faith and strength and he went before the king's gate, risking his life (Esther 4:1-3). Other Jews joined in fasting and intercession within their own provinces. When Mordecai challenged his relative Queen Esther to step in-the-gap on behalf of her people and she responded with fear and reluctance, his response was twofold: to state what God could do to deliver his people and what could befall those who failed to intercede.*
>
> *Mordecai responded with a WARNING which could be applied in our lives today: Failure to intercede might mean ill upon your family, community, church and nation.*

123

"Then Mordecai commanded to answer Esther, Think not with thyself that thou shalt escape in the king's house, more than all the Jews. For if thou altogether hold thy peace at this time, then shall there enlargement and deliverance arise to the Jews from another place; but thou and thy father's house shall be destroyed: and who knows whether thou art come to the kingdom for such a time as this (Esther 4:13, 14- KJV)

Esther's obedience to intercede brought victory to her people and the wicked leader, Haman, was destroyed as his own plots against the people of God backfired (Esther 6:4, 10-12; 7:7-10)!

Constantly In The Place of Watching

One significant role that an intercessor plays is to stand in his watch, watching over the king's business and announcing any threat against the kingdom. Intercessors do this day and night, crying out to God (Isa 62:6-7). The very king who had sent out the edict, when Mordecai discovered a plot against that king, he exposed the plot. Bigthana and Teresh, two of the king's officers who guarded the doorway, had conspired to assassinate King Xerxes. Mordecai jumped in the gap to save the king's life. That was risky too since had these two men found out and got to Mordecai before the king could deal with them, it could have been his demise.

Humility Even After Exaltation

The contrast is so great between Mordecai and Haman. Mordecai basically got Haman's position, a promotion that came into place as a result of King Xerxes honouring him for saving his life and destroying Haman for manipulating him to rise up against the Jews. Mordecai went quickly to take up his position but Haman was grieving bitterly that the king honoured Mordecai.

Then Mordecai returned to the king's gate.
But Haman hurried home, mourning, with his head
covered. (Esther 6:12 – NASV)

Mordecai could have, out of revenge and as the tables had now turned, become a thorn in Haman's side. However, he humbly took the position and began fulfilling his tasks immediately. What an example he was of a true man of God. Imagine, being exalted to the point of a parade put on in the public square and you riding on the king's horse with the nation knowing that the king had selected you for special mention and promotion. How would the average person, even Christians respond? Men of God…men of prayer can take a leaf out of Mordecai's book. The man that God desires can keep on his cloak of humility wherever God places him; whomever he is with; whatever his function or the role he plays. That man can reflect the true nature of God whether he is in an insignificant or exalted position.

God always seeks for a man through whom He can do exploits and God is always on the watch, constantly looking out for people who are totally committed to Him. He sees the heart and he knows those who are not perfect, not without fault, not righteous in their own eyes. He sees those who will allow Him to prove Himself through them. He seeks for those who will allow Him to be strong in them being fully cognizant of their own weakness. He seeks for the one who is constantly seeking to cultivate the heart of God and the mind of Christ within his own life. He is looking for a heart that is completely His.

For the eyes of the Lord move to and fro throughout
the earth that He may strongly support those whose
heart is completely His [2 Chron 16:9 - NASB]

Devon:

So as men of God let us follow the examples of David and Mordecai in daily being the men that God desires. Imperfect men, weak men, but men who find their strength in panting after God as the deer pants after the water brooks. Men who desire what God desires and delight themselves in Him. Such are the men that God is seeking. Will you be one?

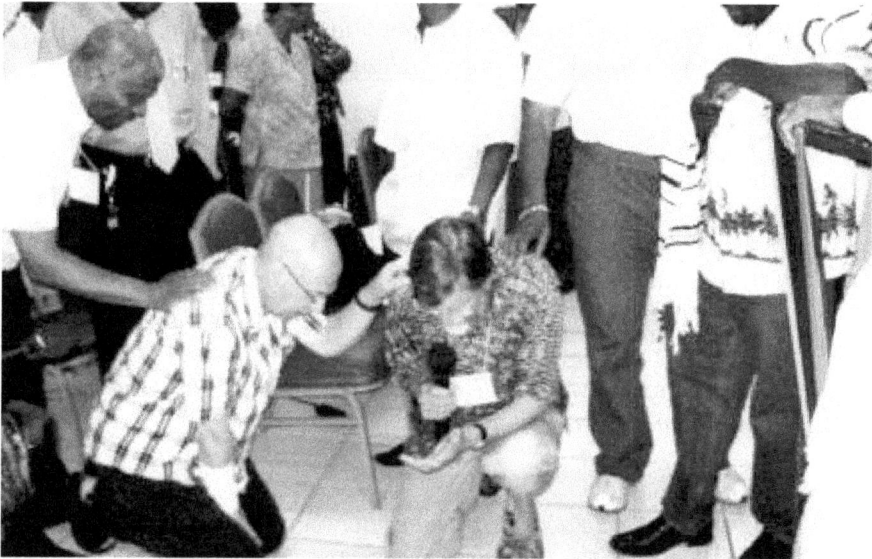

Male representatives from Europe repenting in-the-gap and praying for the colonized nations at the Caribbean Prayer Summit, Ocho Rios, Jamaica

Bibliography

1. Munroe, Myles. (2001). UNDERSTANDING THE PURPOSE AND POWER OF MEN: a book for men and the women who love them., New Kensington, PA: Whitaker House (p 170)

2. Gray, John. Men Are from Mars, Women Are from Venus: The Classic Guide to Understanding the Opposite Sex. (1992). USA: HarperCollins Publishers.

3. Joel, Daphna. (2015). An article published online in The Guardian. [***http://www.theguardian.com/science/2015***]

4. Online article, *A way to encourage men to pray*, [http://cuyahogavalleychurch.blogspot.com]

5. Miglioratti, Phil. *Pastors' Strategies for Mobilizing Men to Pray, [Phil Miglioratti, http://www.churchleaders.com]*

6. Luhrmann, Tanya. May 7, 2012. *Why Women Hear God More Than Men* [www.christianitytoday.com]

7. *Gender & the Brain: Differences between Women & Men,* [http://www.fitbrains.com/blog/women-men-brains]

8. Harbajan, Maria L. 2015. *ARISE...Intercessors ARISE! A Manual For the Birthing, Calling, Training and Restoration of Prayer Warriors*. USA:Outskirts Press, Inc.

9. Grohol, John M. Article: 10 *Reasons You Can't Say How You Feel. [http://psychcentral.com/lib/10-reasons-you-cant-say-how-you-feel/]*

10. *Staats Reiss, Dombeck, Natalie and Mark, Online Article: "Suicide Statistics" [https://www.mentalhelp.net/articles/suicide-statistics]*

11. *Online Article: "MEN IN FAMILIES and Family Policy in a Changing World" [http://www.un.org/esa/socdev/family/docs/men-in-families.]*

12. Luhrmann, Tanya. MAY 7, 2012. Online article in *Christianity Today*, [www.christianitytoday.com]

About The Authors

DEVON & MARIA HARBAJAN are both national leaders in the Prayer Movement in Jamaica and are the leaders of the National Intercessory Prayer Network of Jamaica / Prayer Centre of the Caribbean (NIPNOJ/ P-COC) with the mandate of raising an army of intercessors for God. They train adults, youth and children.

Rev. Devon Harbajan is a telecommunications engineer by profession. He has been involved especially with training children since he was in his teens. His passion is prayer and missions. He is currently Executive Chairman of NIPNOJ/P-COC. He has been involved in ministry for over 30 years.

Rev. Dr. Maria Harbajan is author of the book, *ARISE...Intercessors ARISE! A Manual For the Birthing, Calling, Training and Restoration of Prayer Warriors.* **Outskirts Press, Inc., 2015**. President and CEO of NIPNOJ/P-COC). She is involved in the ministry of intercession for over 30 years. She is host of a radio programme, "ARISE AND BUILD JAMAICA", calling the nation to rise up in prayer and action to build the Kingdom of God. This is aired on LOVE FM in Jamaica, WI.

Mr & Mrs Harbajan have both known Jesus as their personal Saviour from their youth. They have both acquired certification professionally and within the Kingdom of God from various institutions . Mrs. Harbajan has been in full-time ministry since 1991. She is also a member of the Executive Team of the International Prayer Council. Founder and senior counsellor of the OASIS Counselling Services, she seeks to restore individuals and families to their God-given purpose and to assist Christian businesses to function under God.

They speak at conferences, camps, schools, churches, etc. They cover a variety of topics including Family and Marital Relationships,

Intercession, Spiritual Warfare, Stress Management, Team-building, Issues Involving Young People, and personal issues that affect people in the workplace. Their ministry has taken them to Africa, Asia, Europe, the Caribbean, Central and South America.

Both are involved in Missions, teaching pastors and other leaders on the Mission field. They are members at the Portmore Gospel Assembly, St. Catherine, Jamaica, and have a son DeMario Samuel.

CONTACT INFORMATION:

DEVON & MARIA HARBAJAN
National Intercessory Prayer Network of Jamaica /
Prayer Centre of the Caribbean
53 Church Street, Kingston Jamaica WI
Call 876-806-4921 or 876-967-4041 (office)
E-mail address: mardevharb@cwjamaica.com /
prayernet@cwjamaica.com

www.ingramcontent.com/pod-product-compliance
Lightning Source LLC
Chambersburg PA
CBHW060805050426

42449CB00008B/1552